This coloring book belongs to

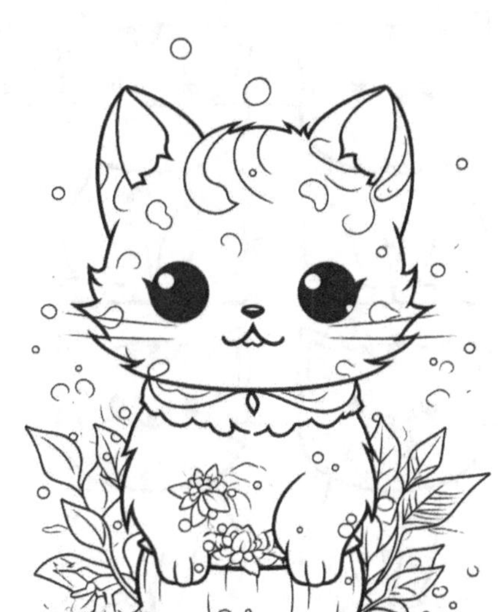 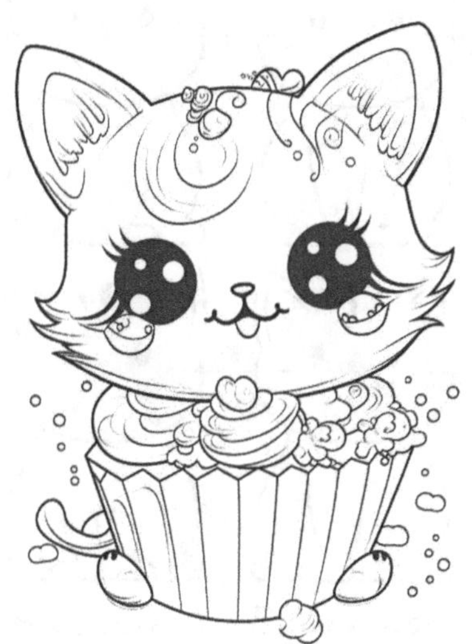

Love this Coloring book?
Want to show off your masterpiece?
Do you want your art displayed on our website?

1. Take a picture of a finished coloring page
2. Scan the QR Code to go to our website
3. Upload the photo of your finished coloring page

OR

Use #happytimesbooks or mention us
@happytimesbooks on Instragram to
have it displayed on our front page

No registration required

If you are under 18 please get a parents permission

https://happytimesbooks.com/pages/customer-art

Color Test Page

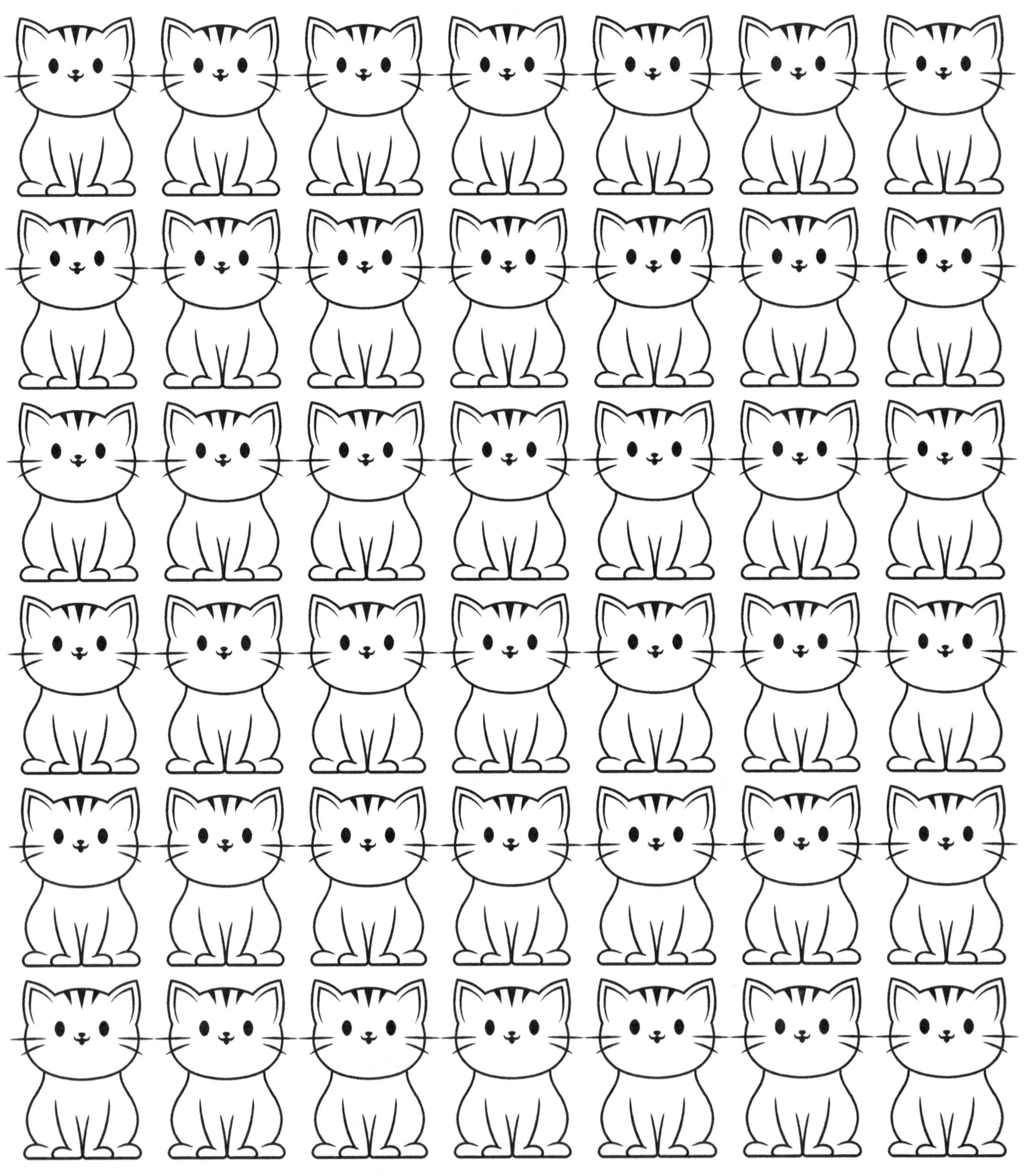

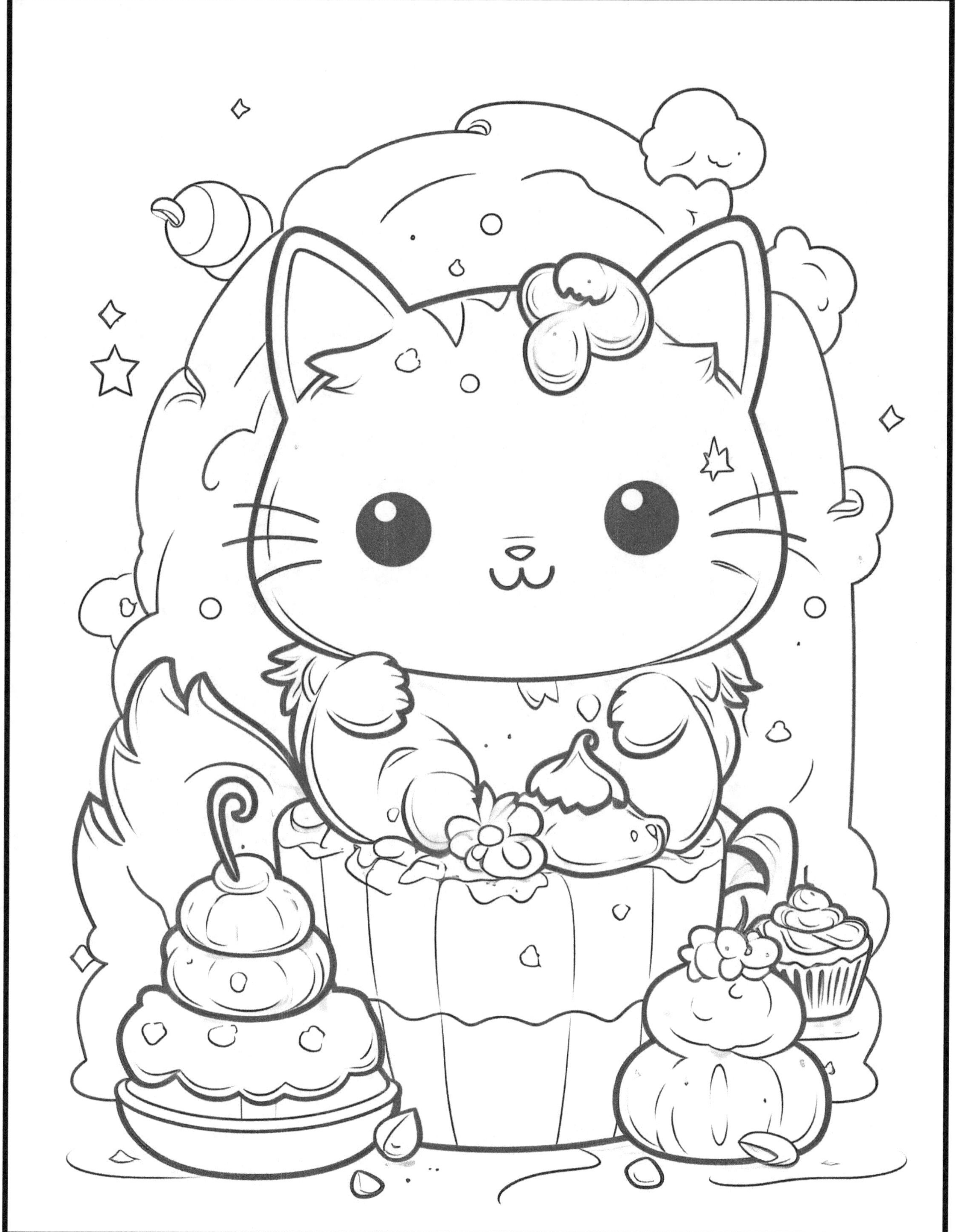

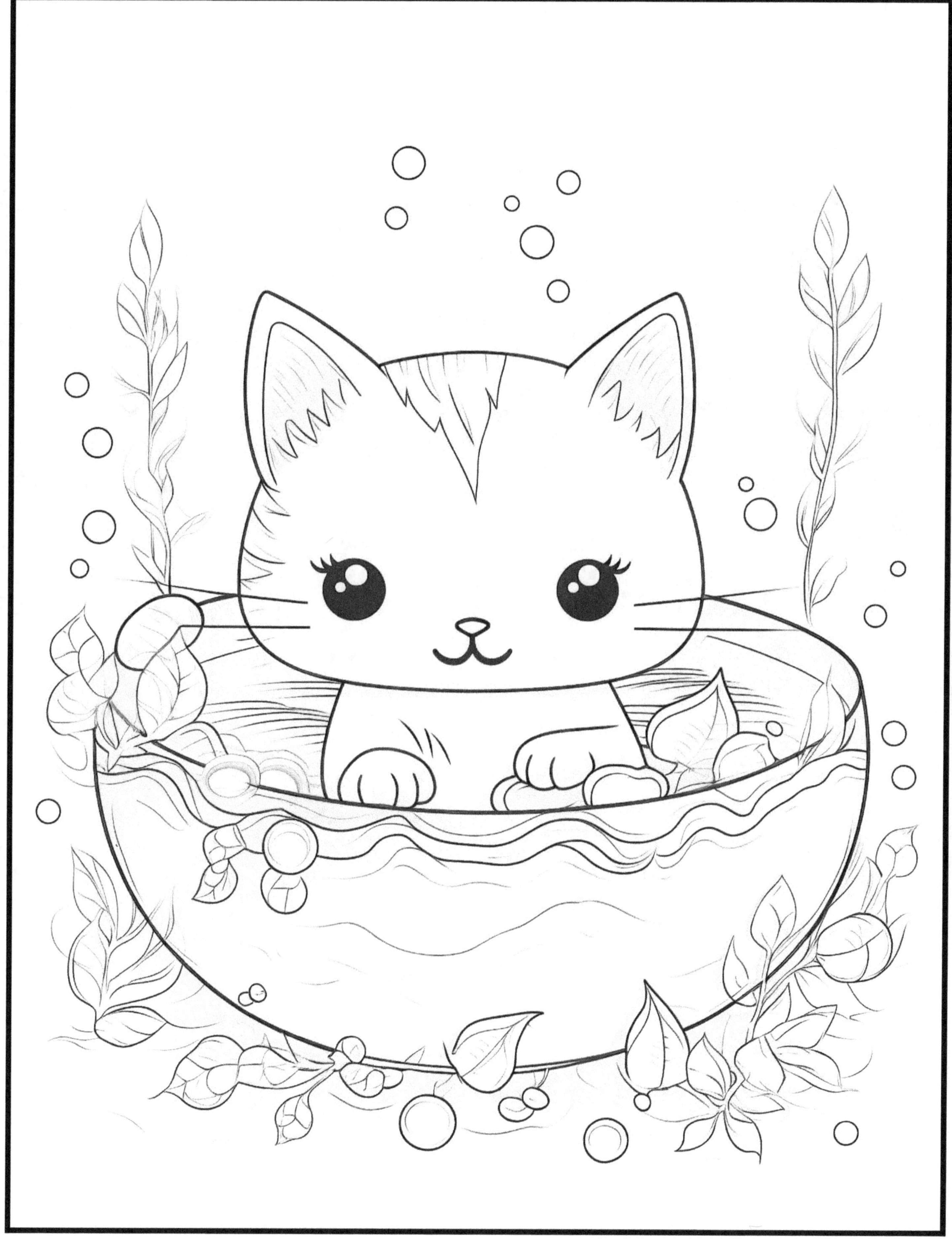

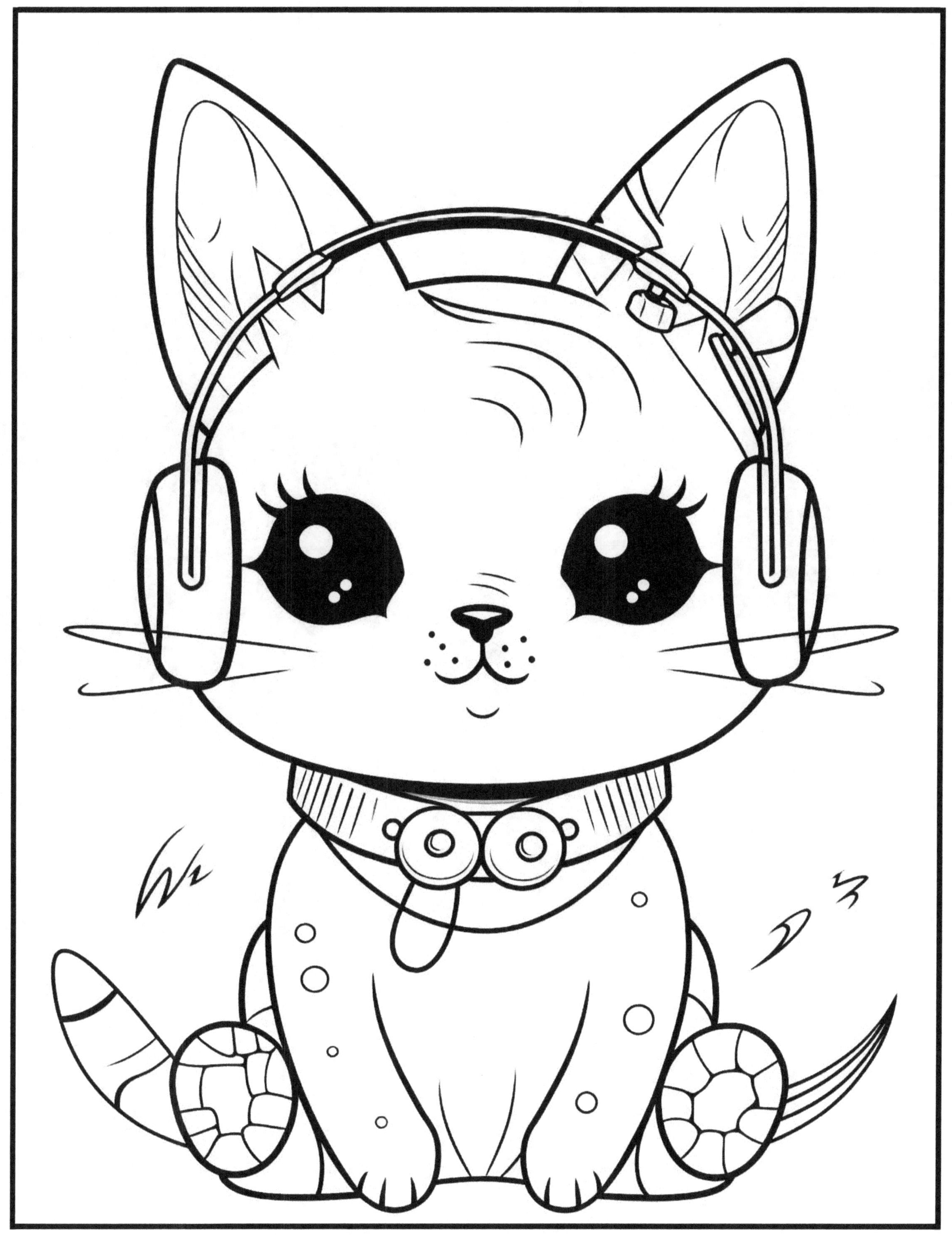

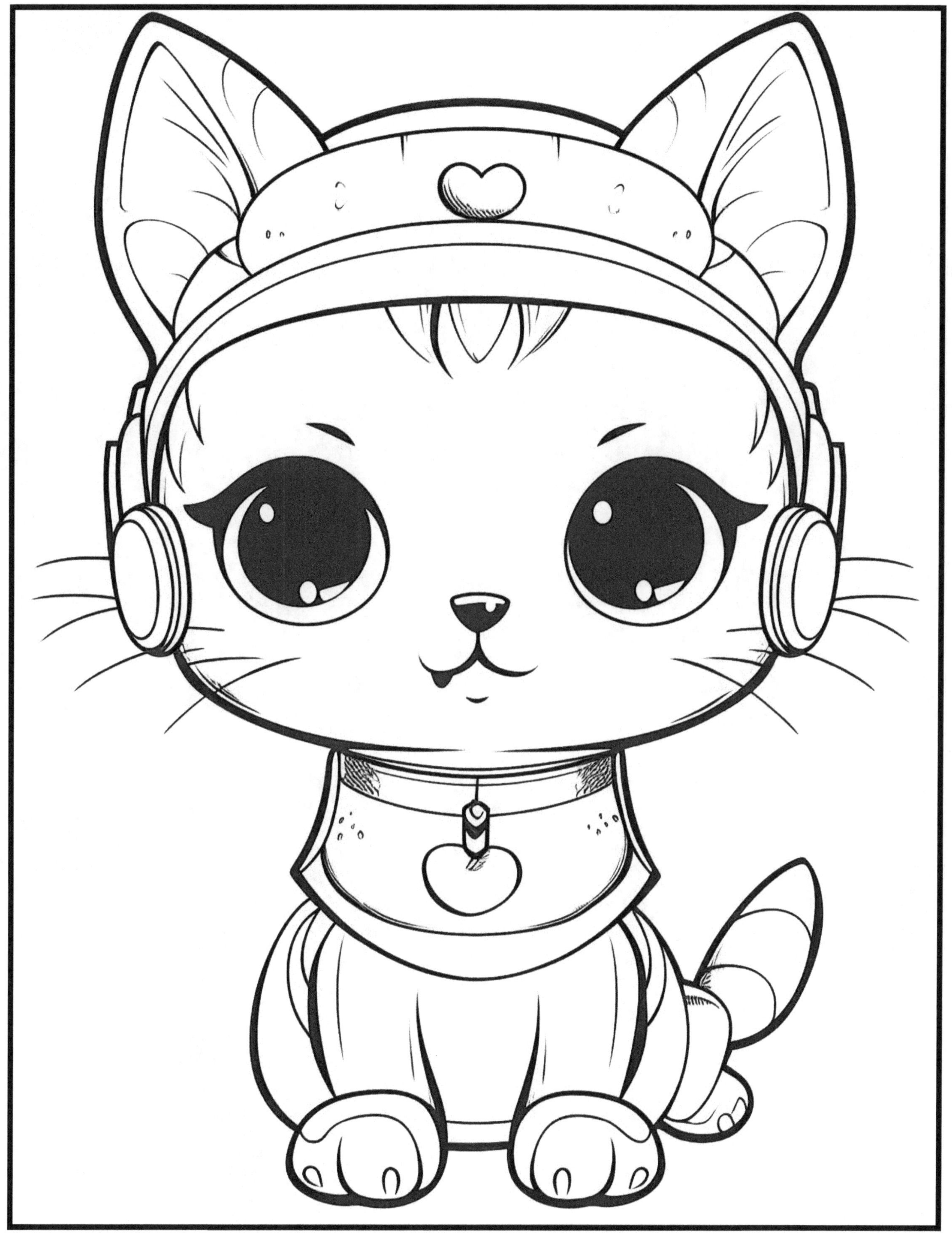

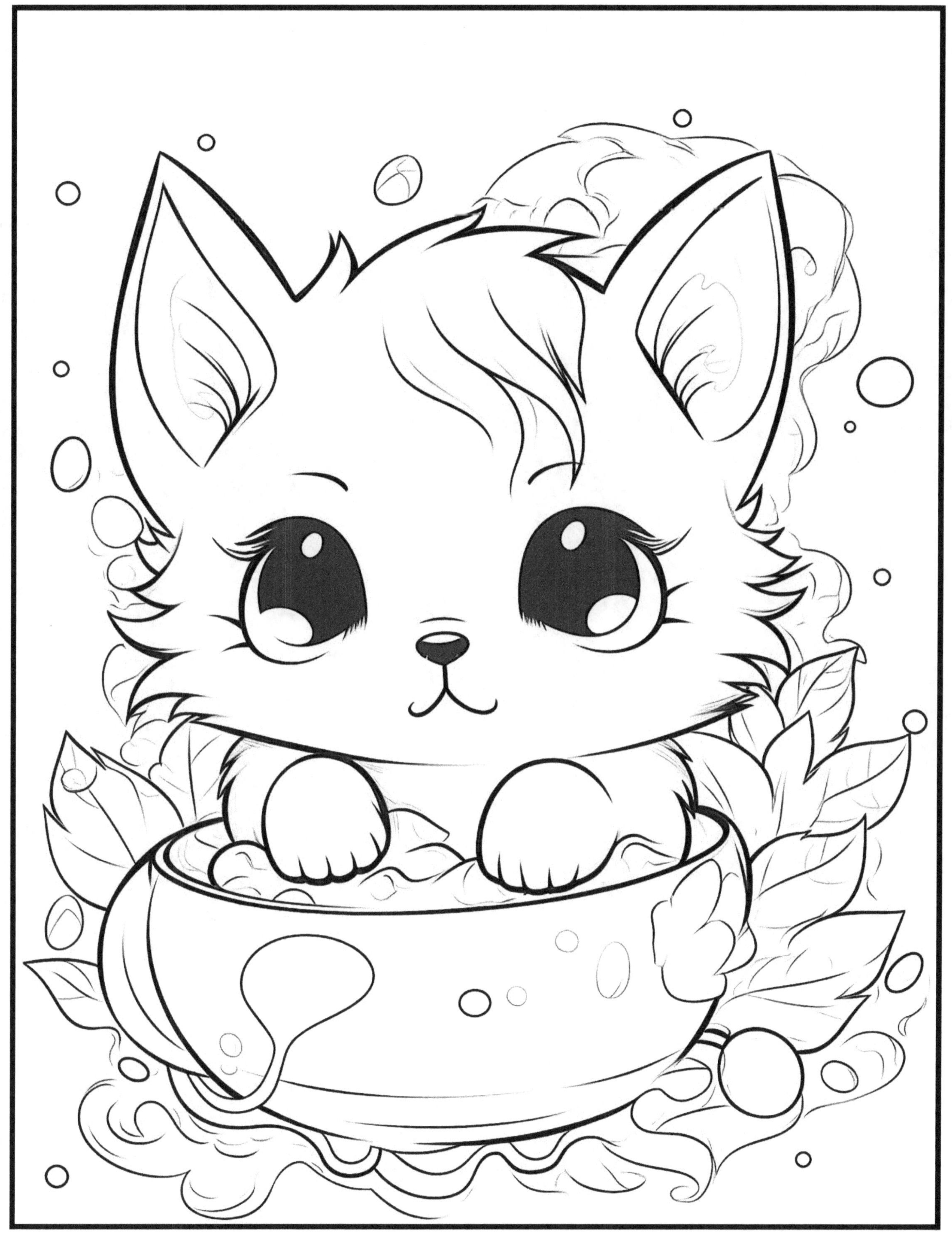

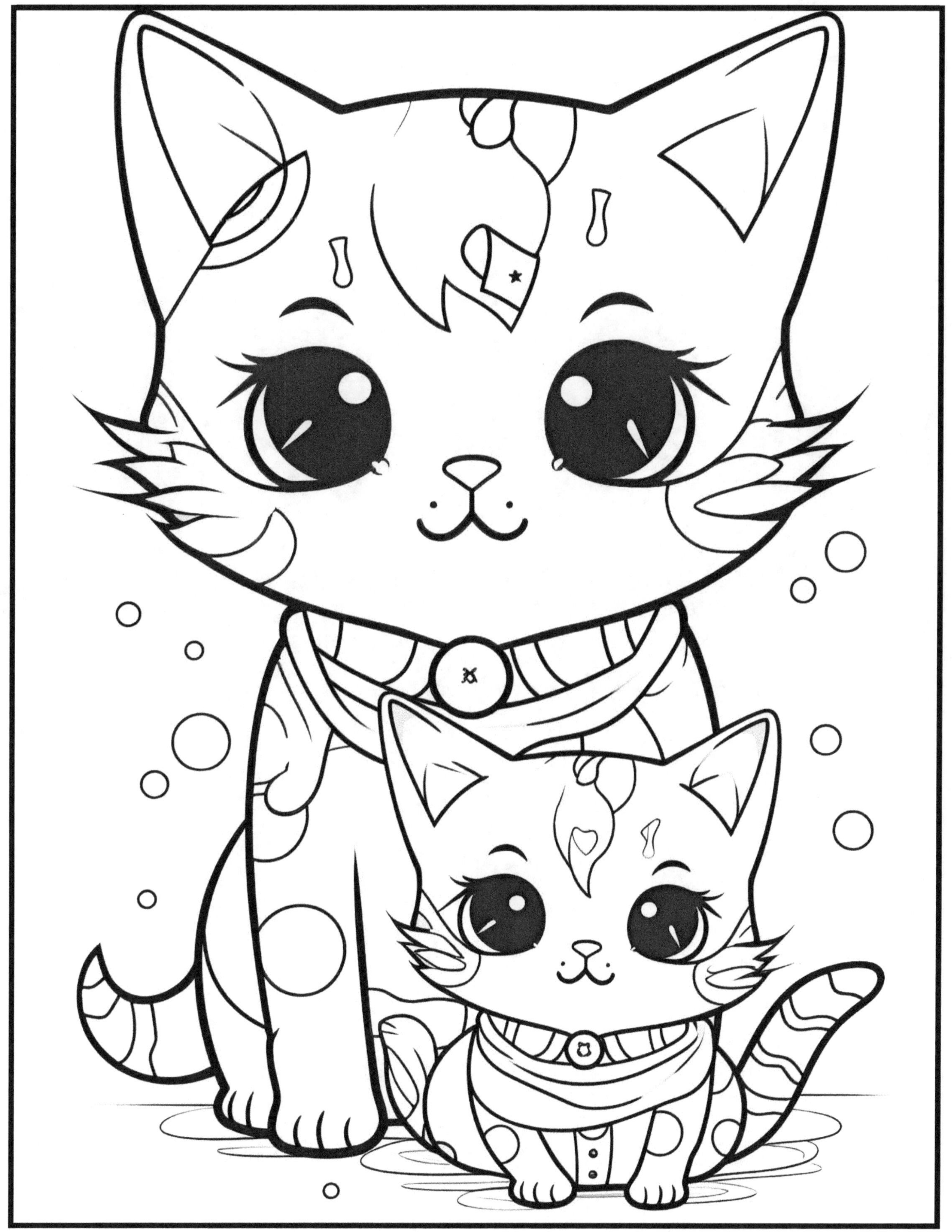

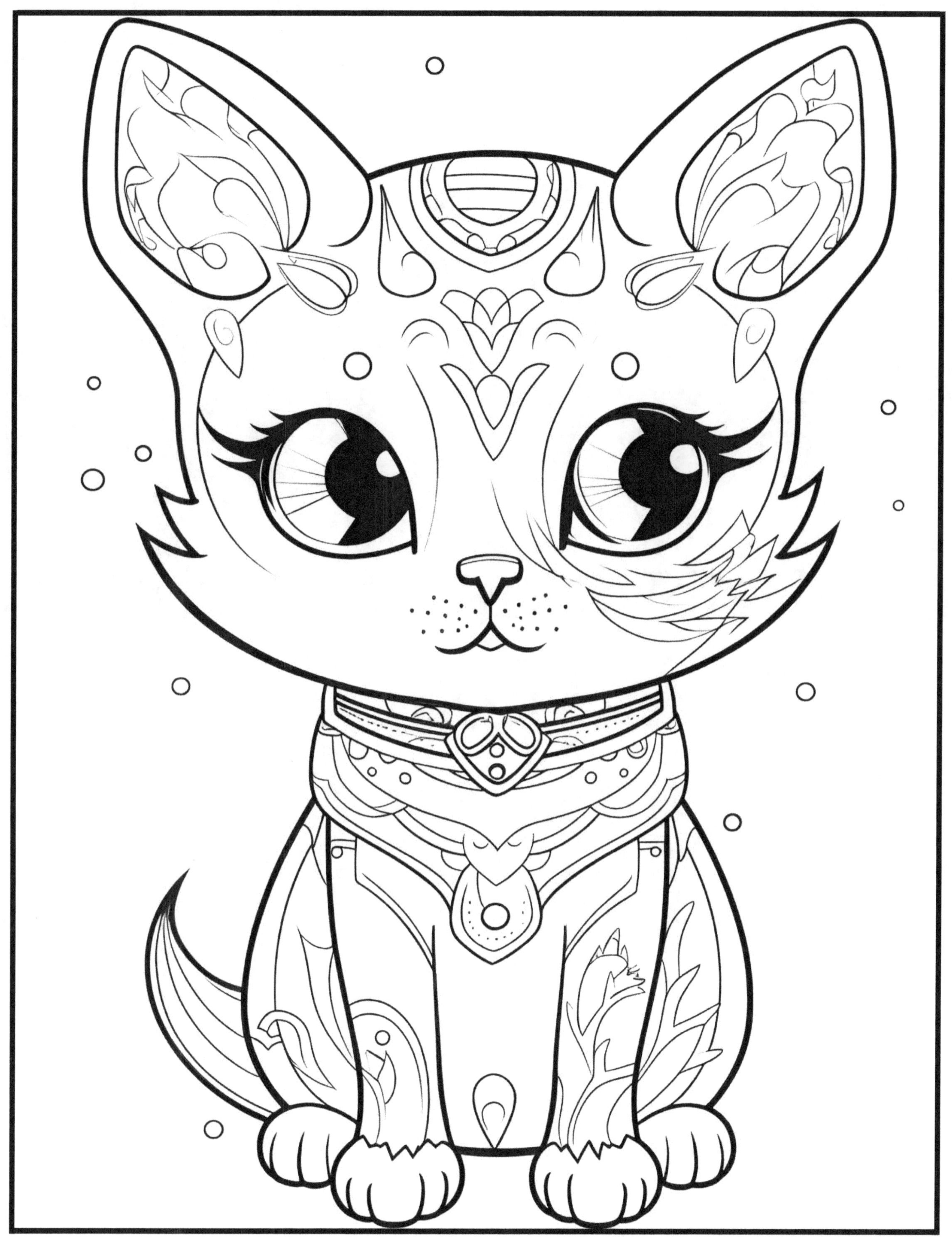

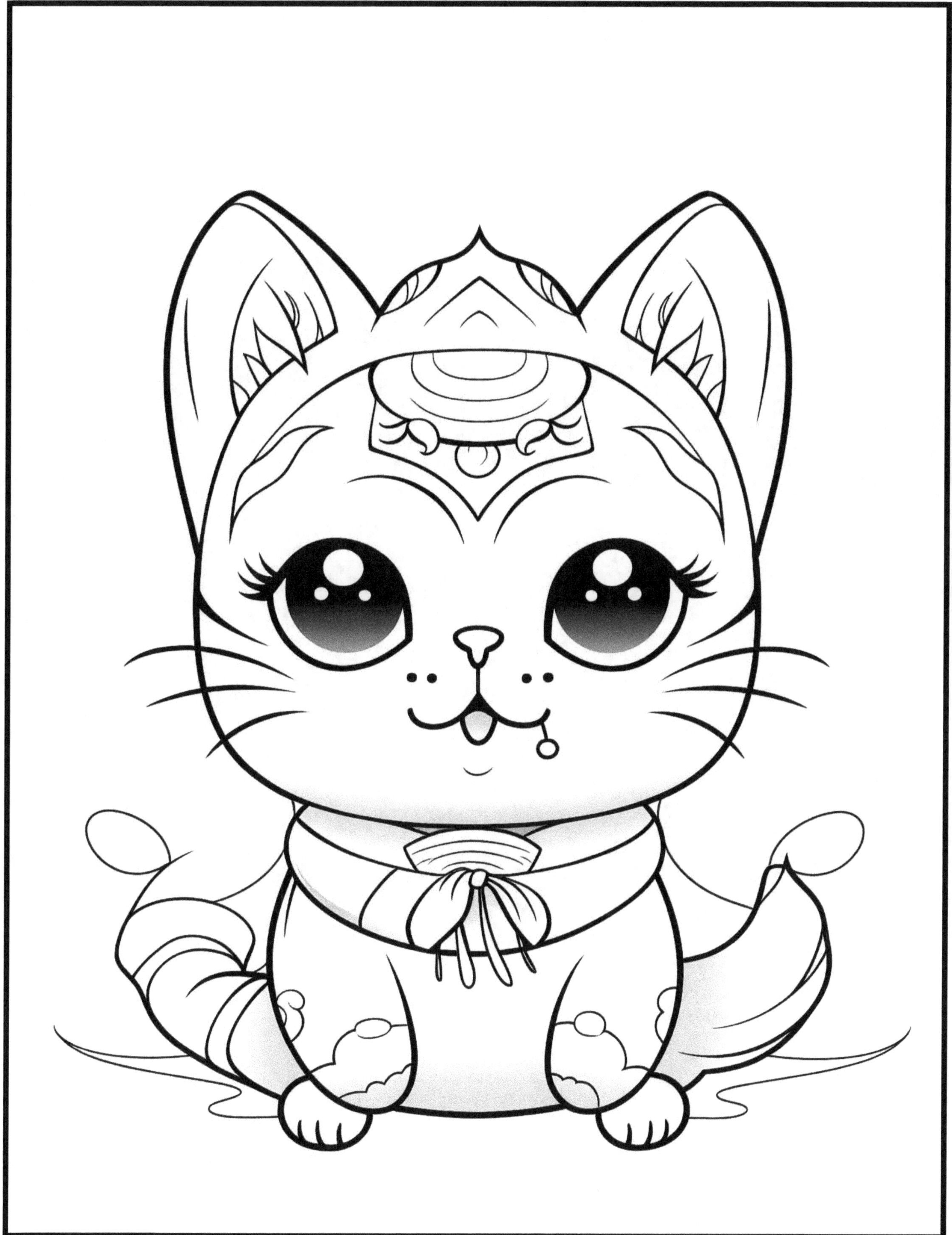

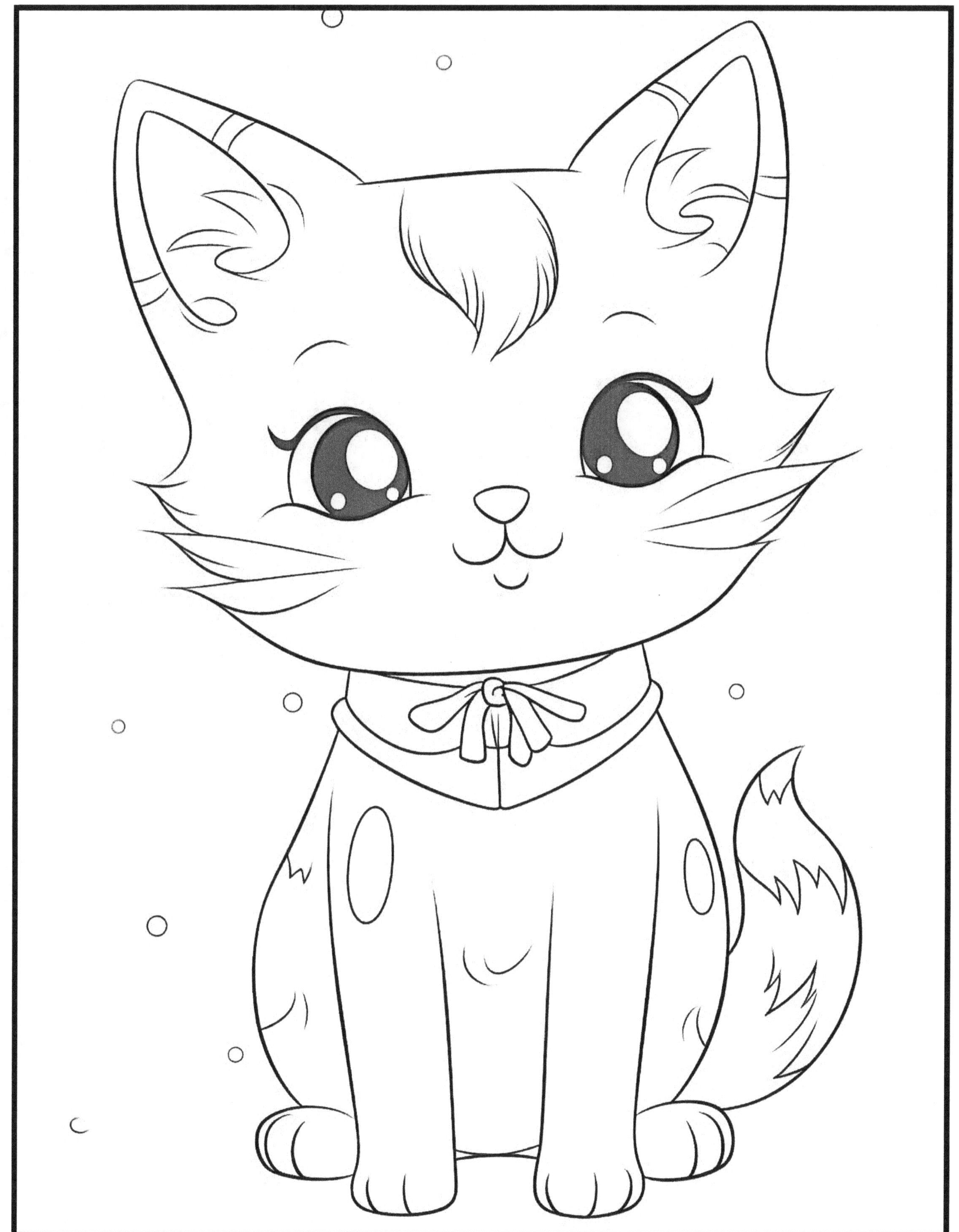

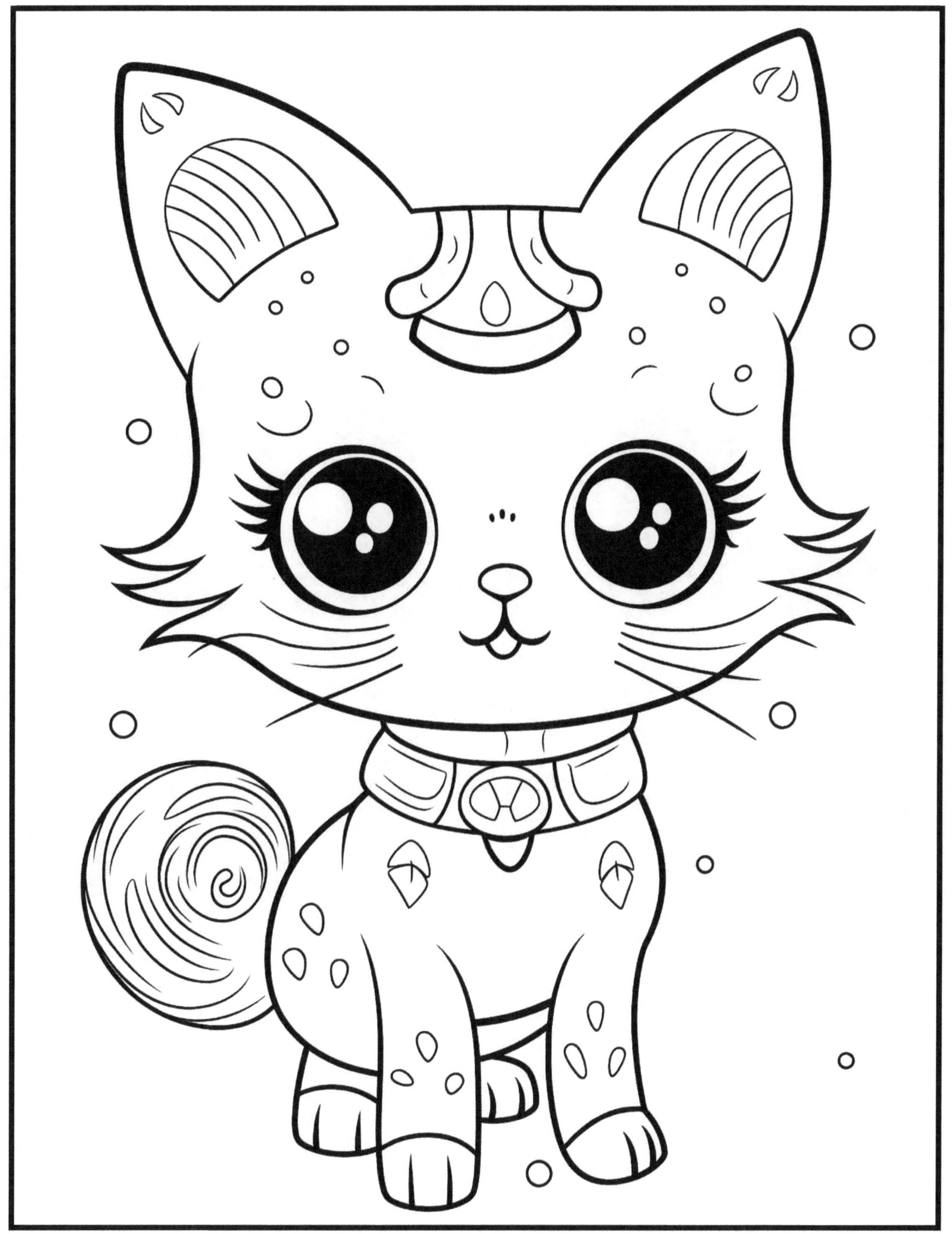

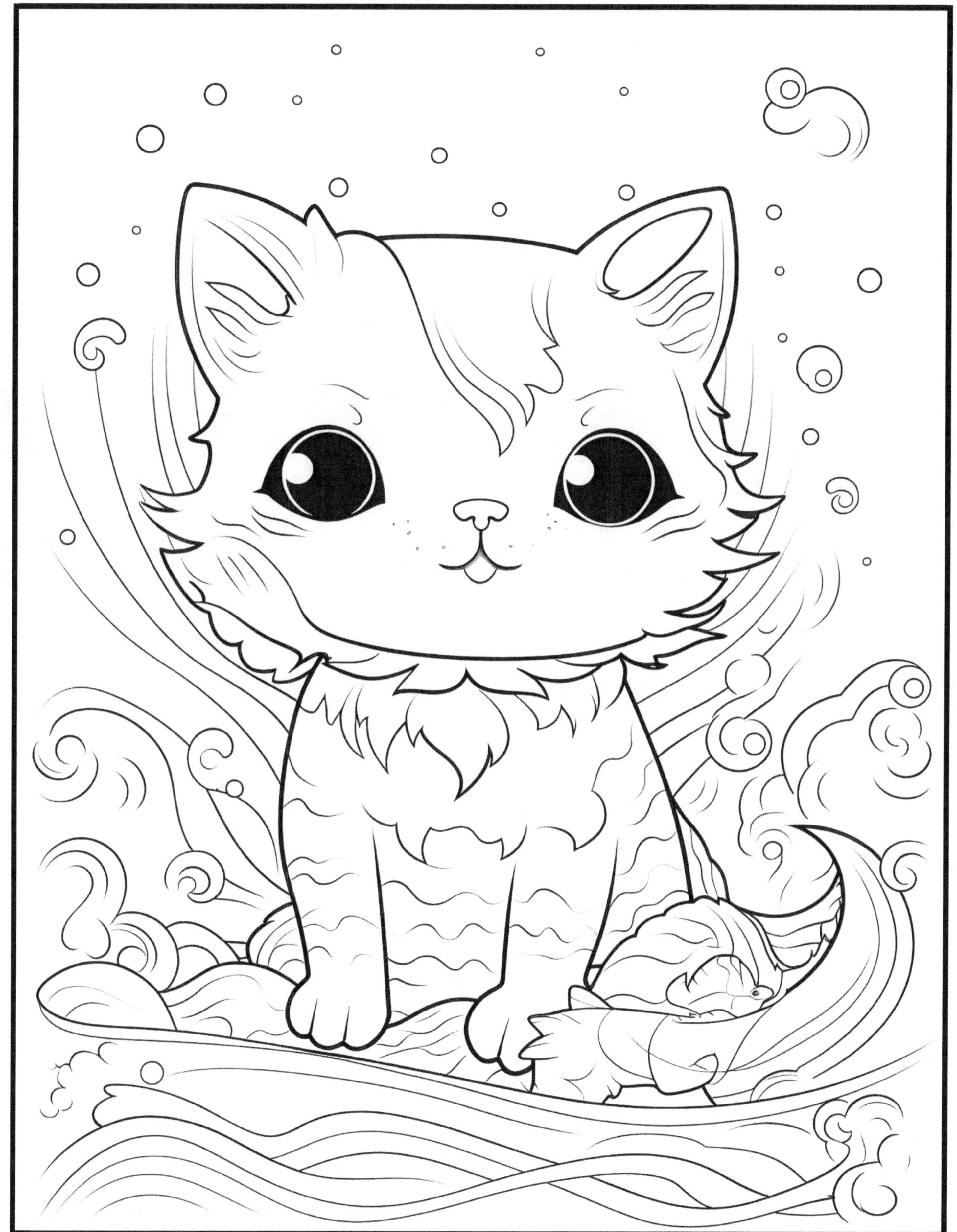

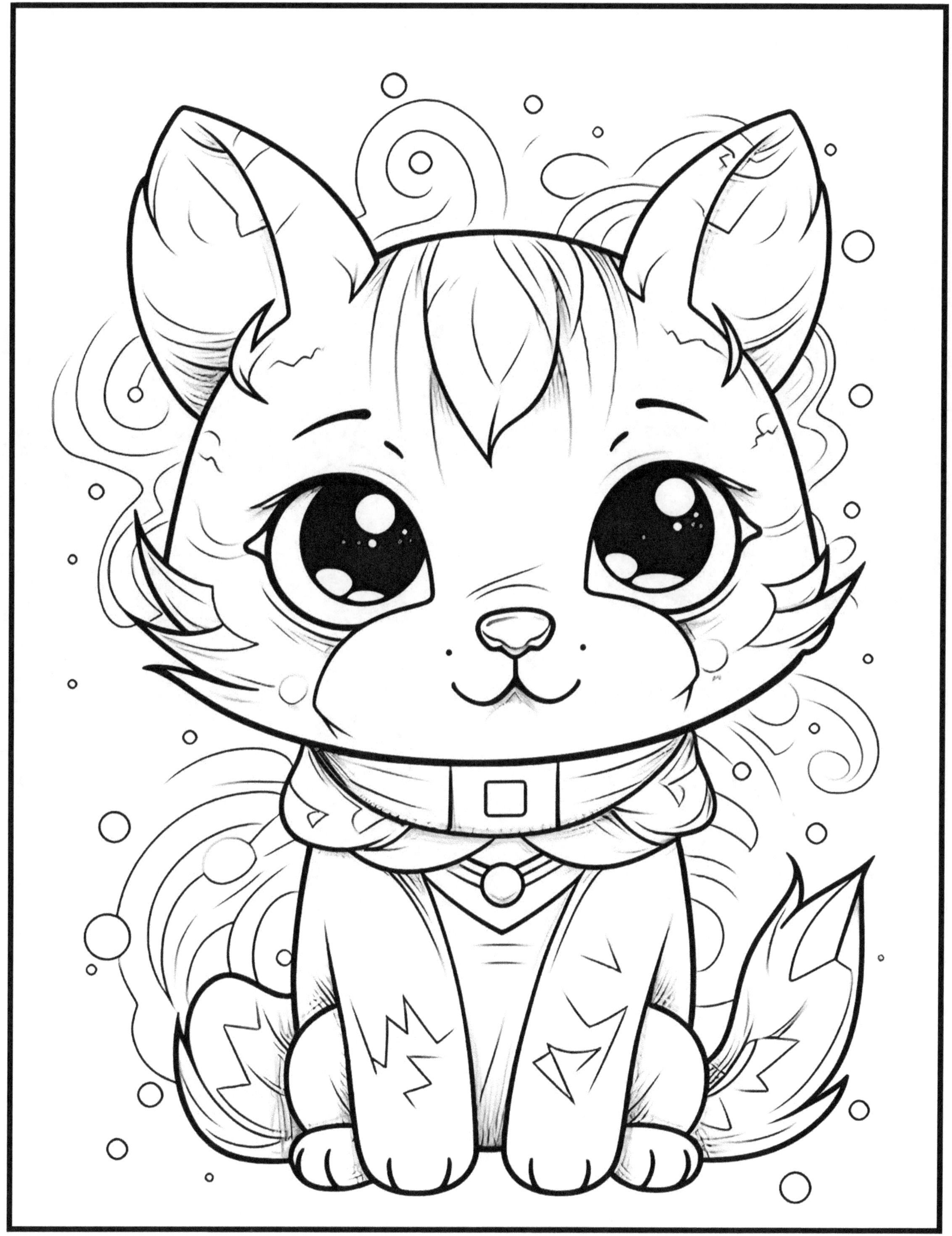

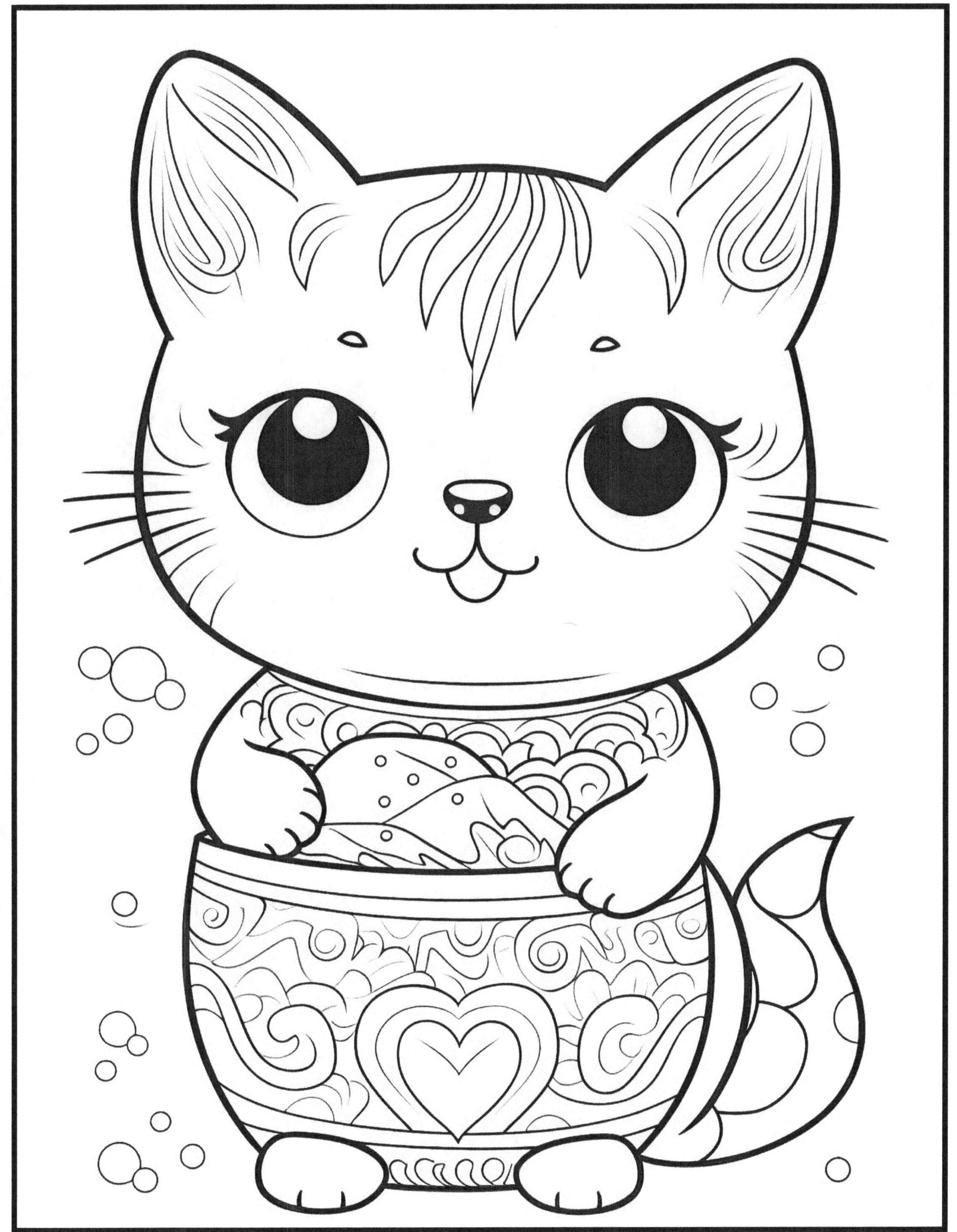

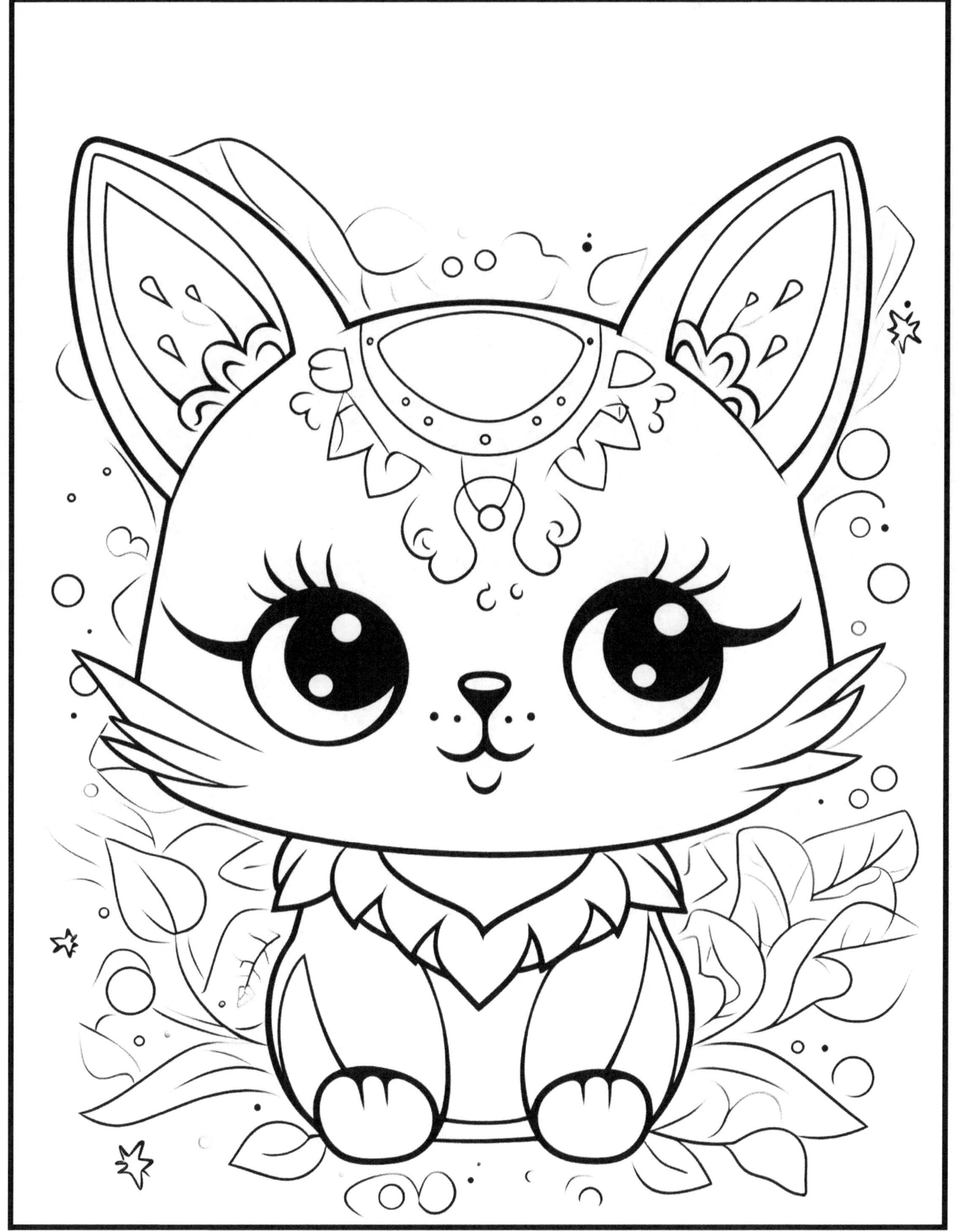

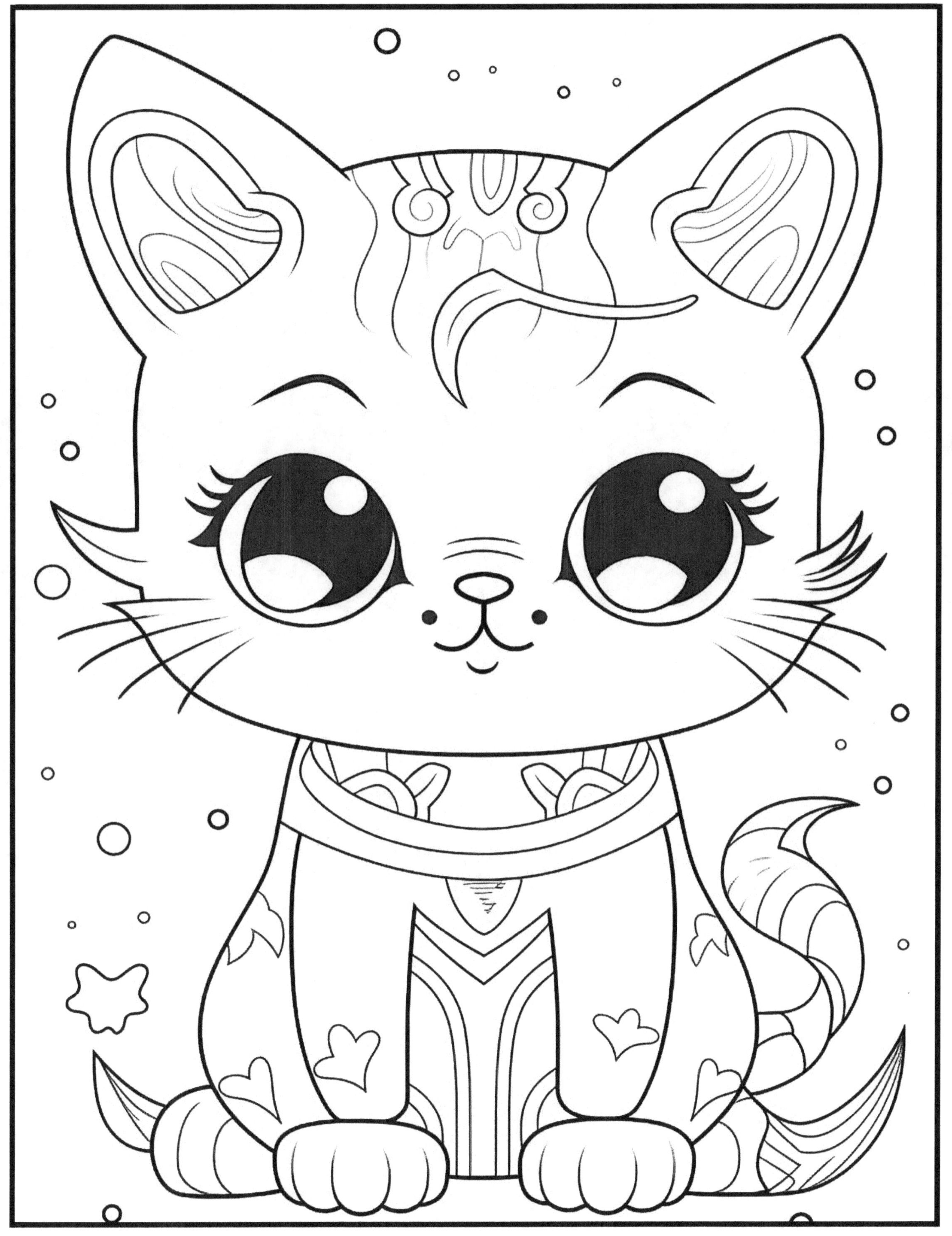

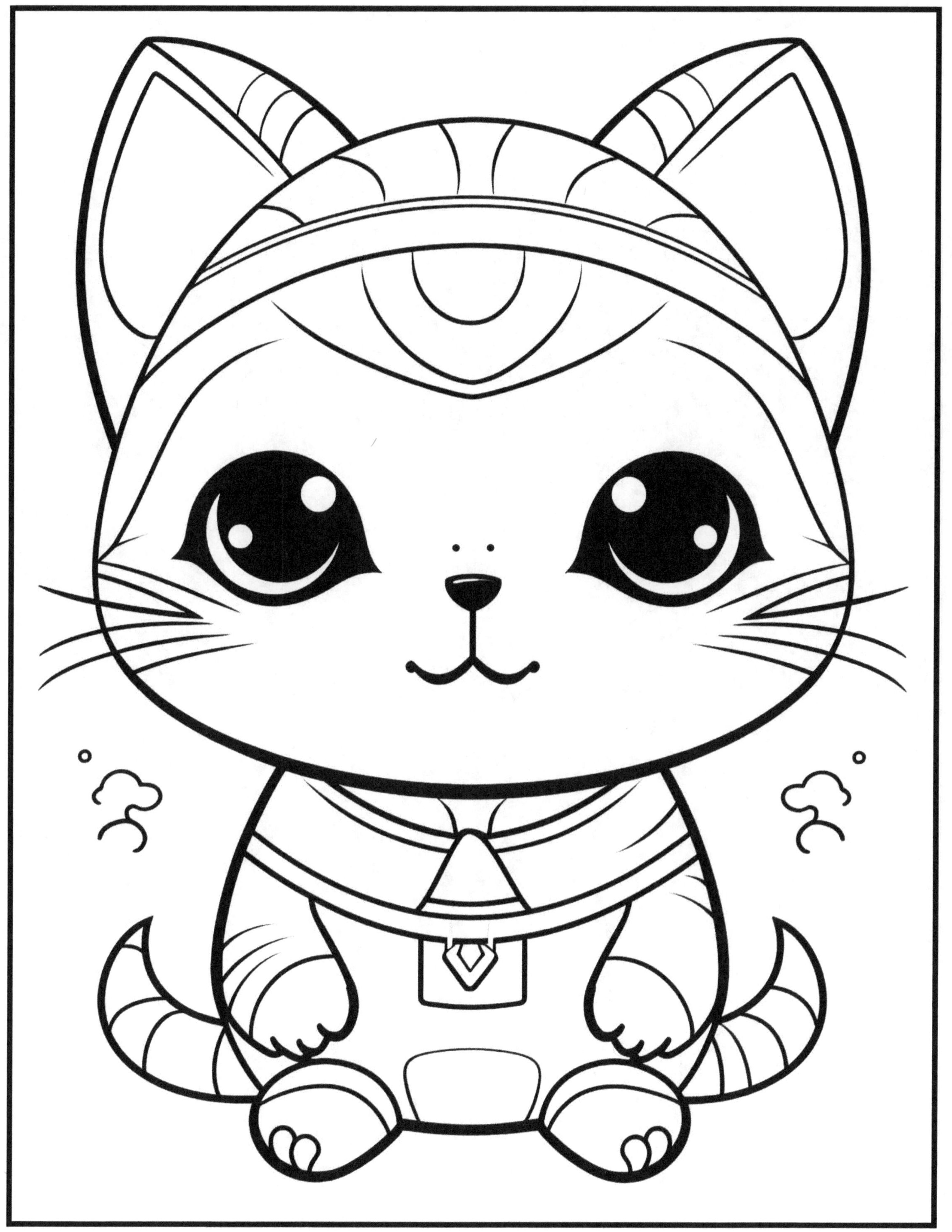

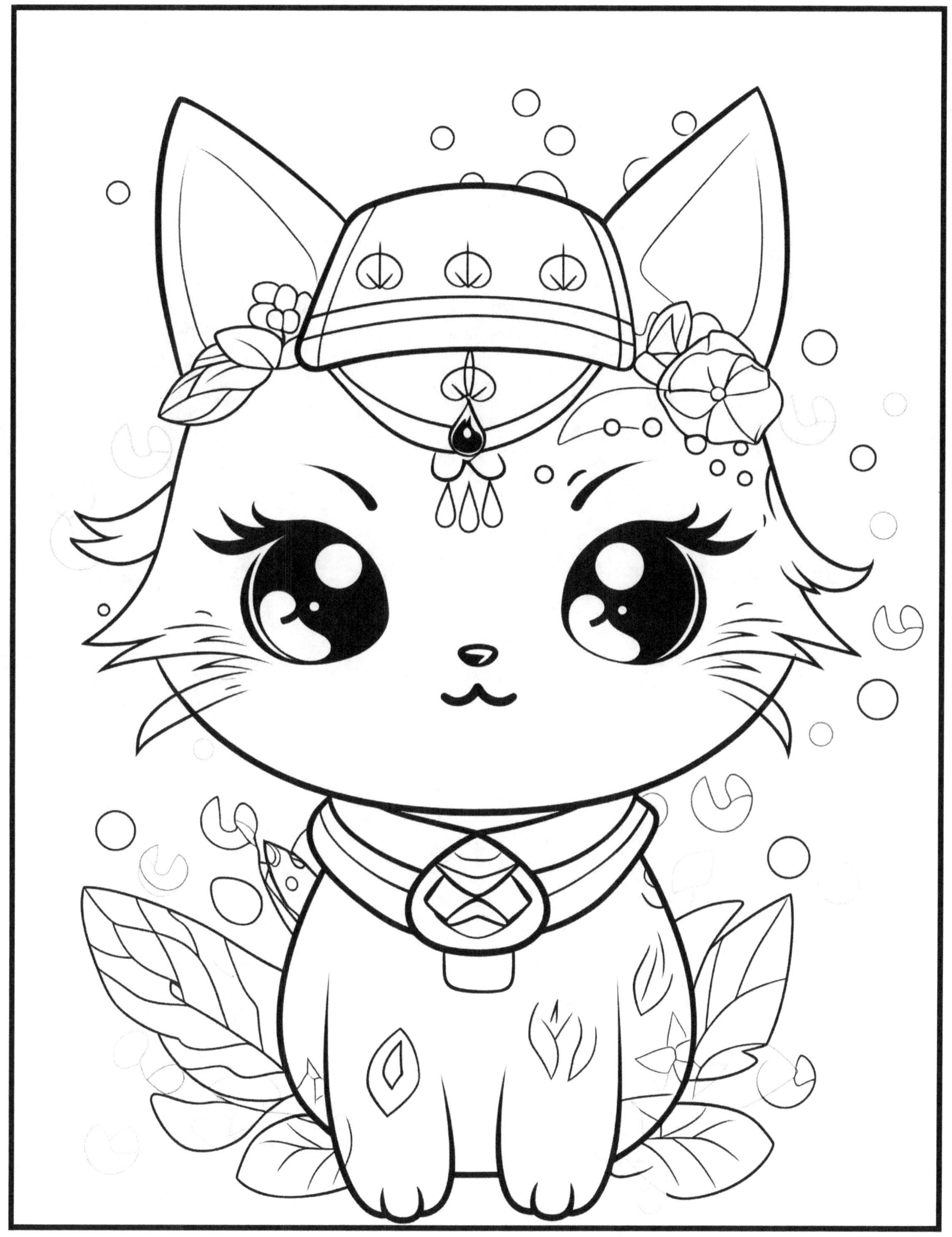

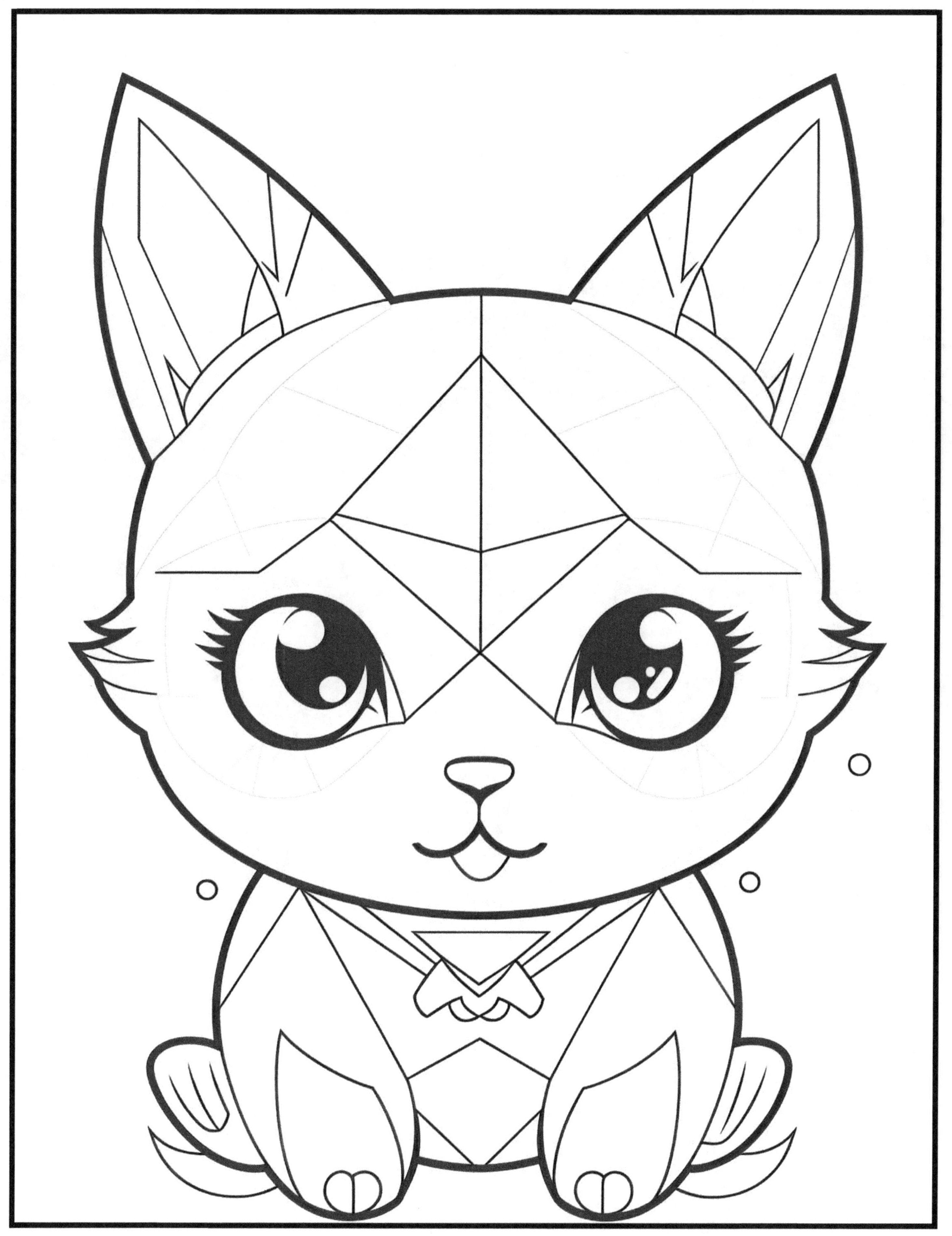

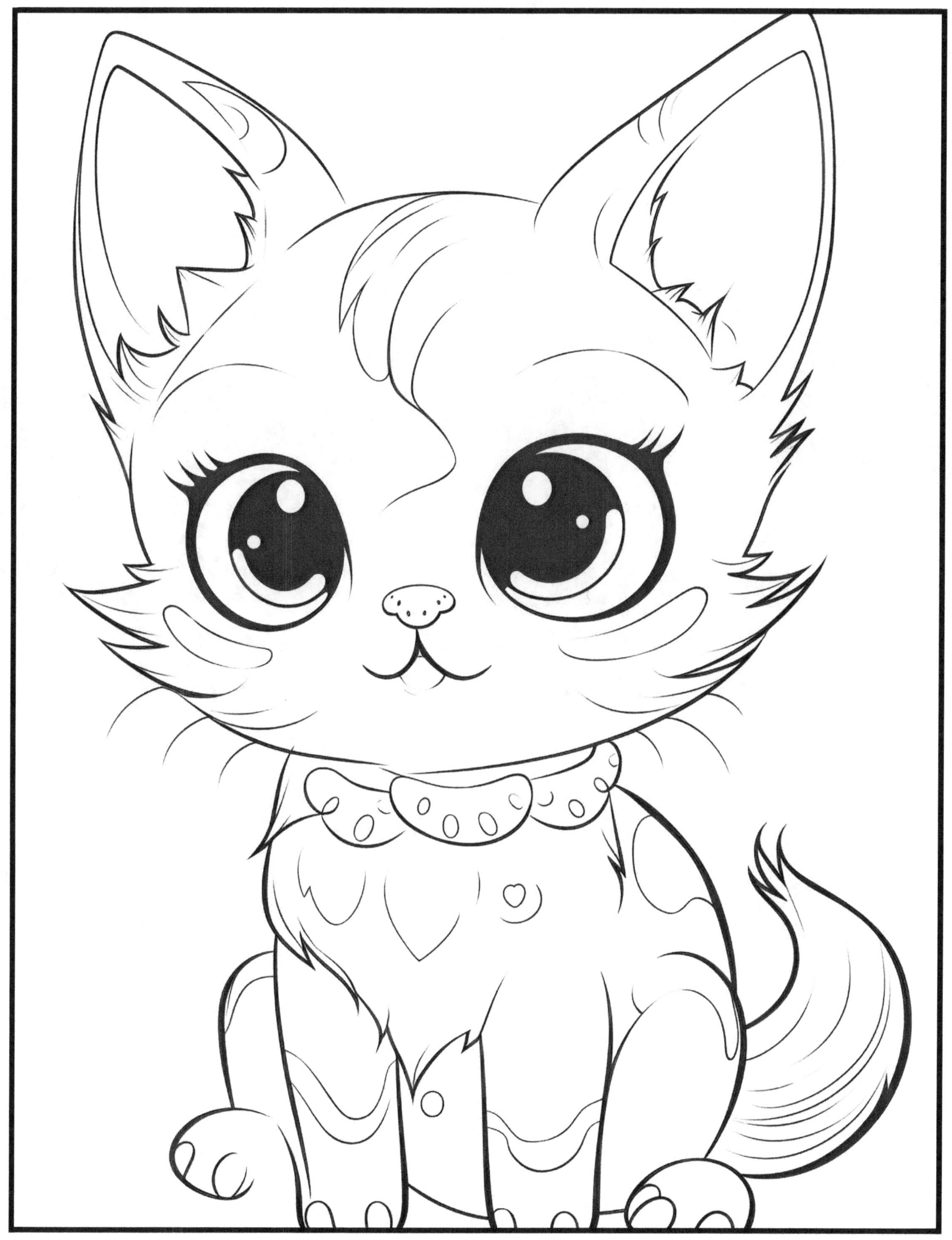

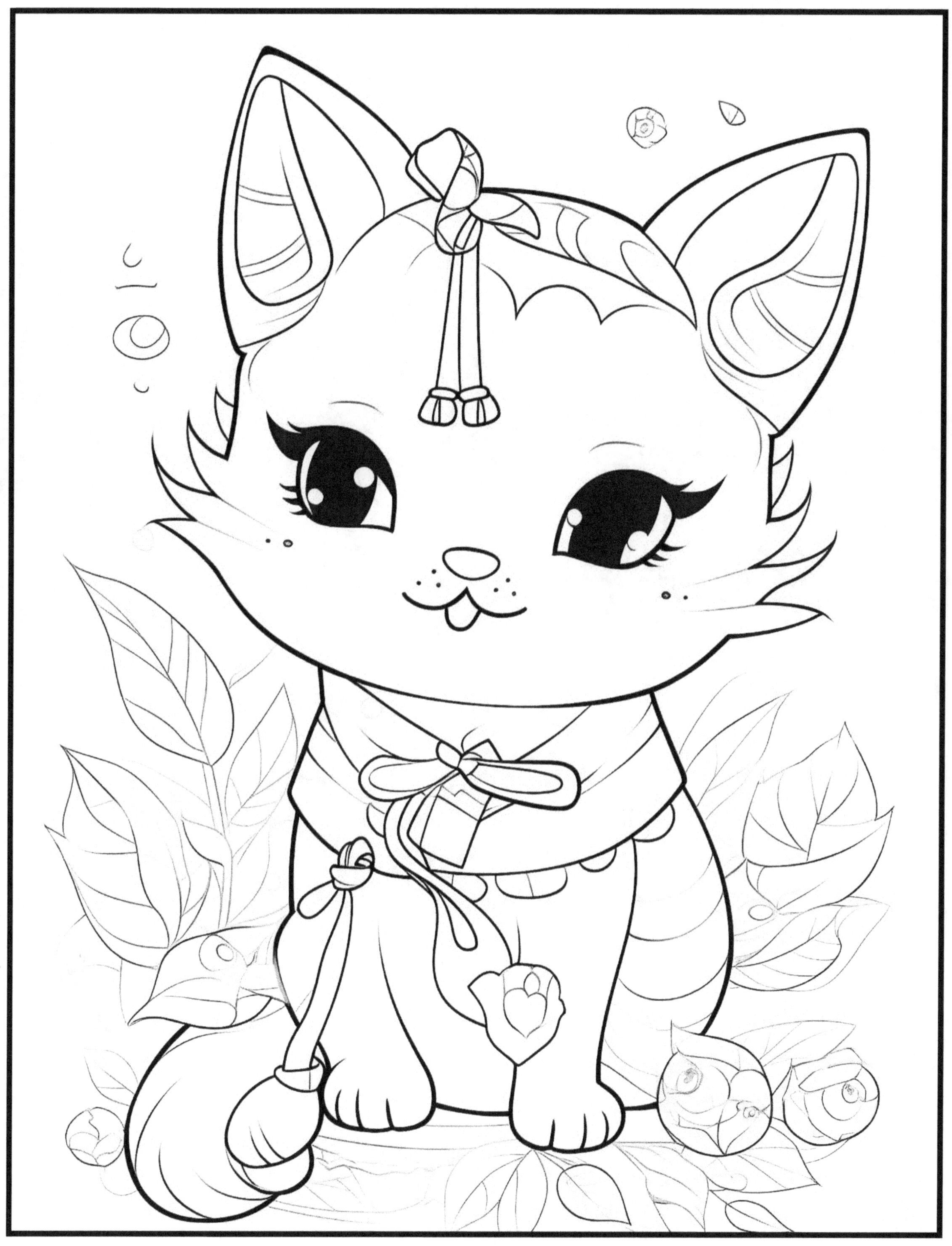

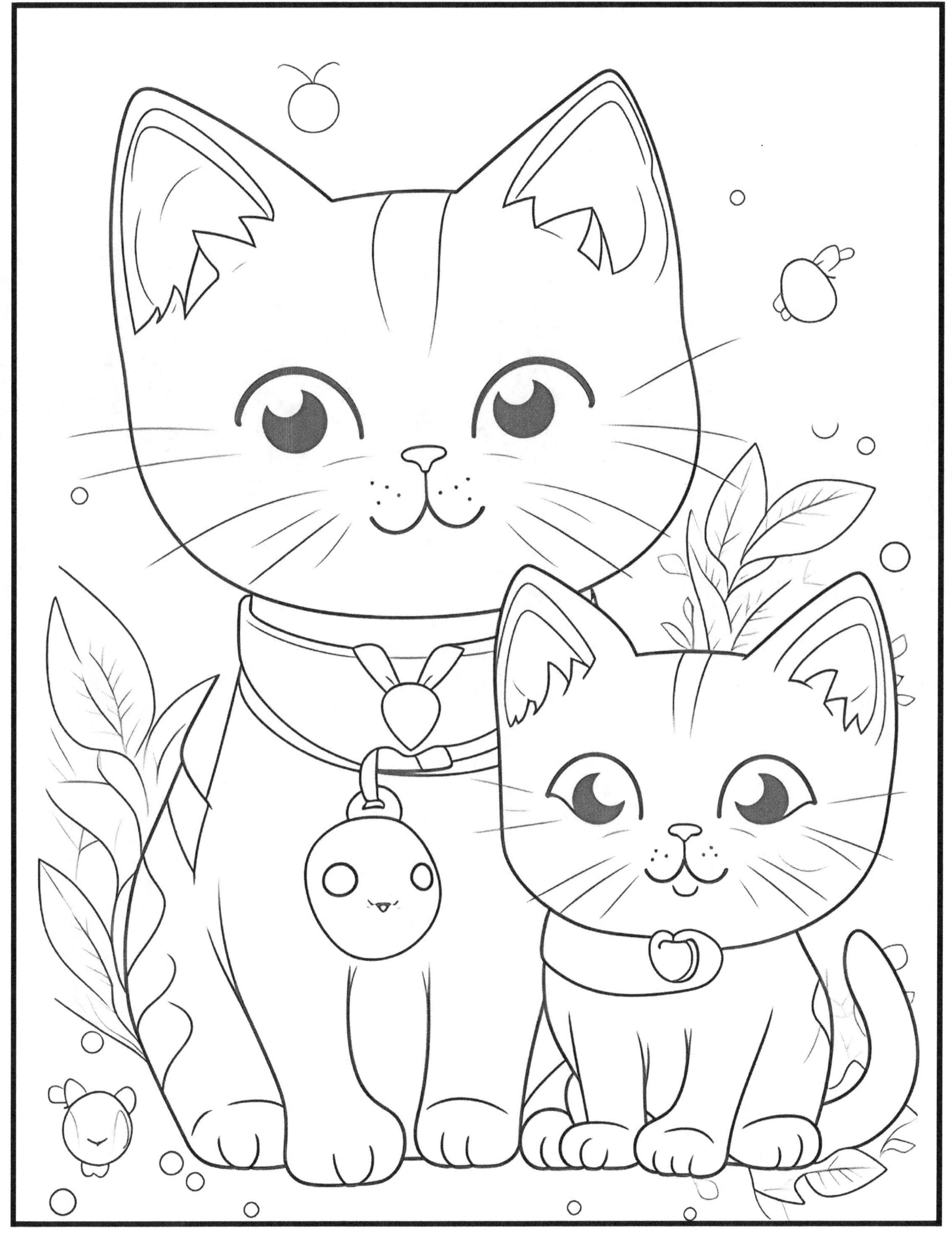

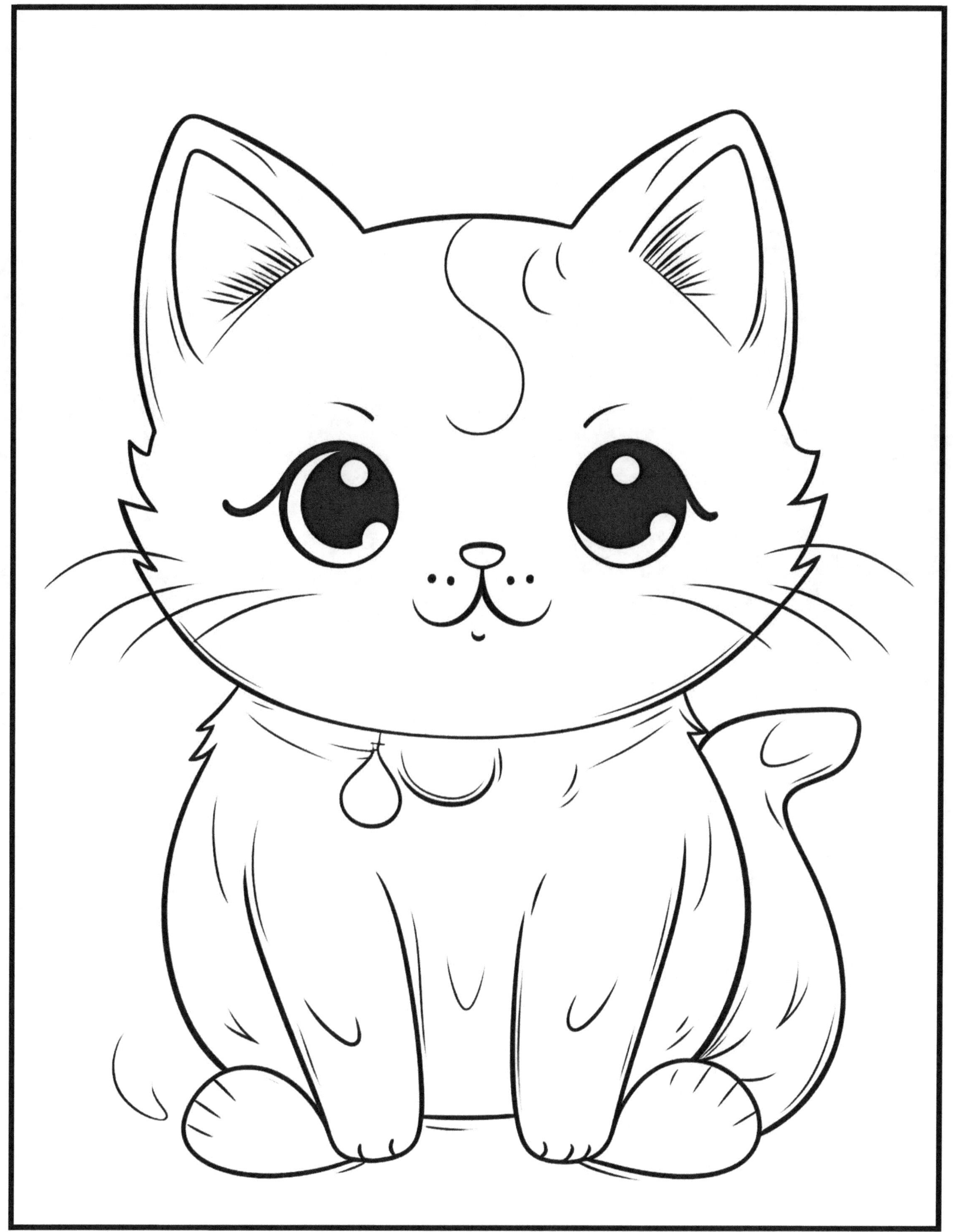

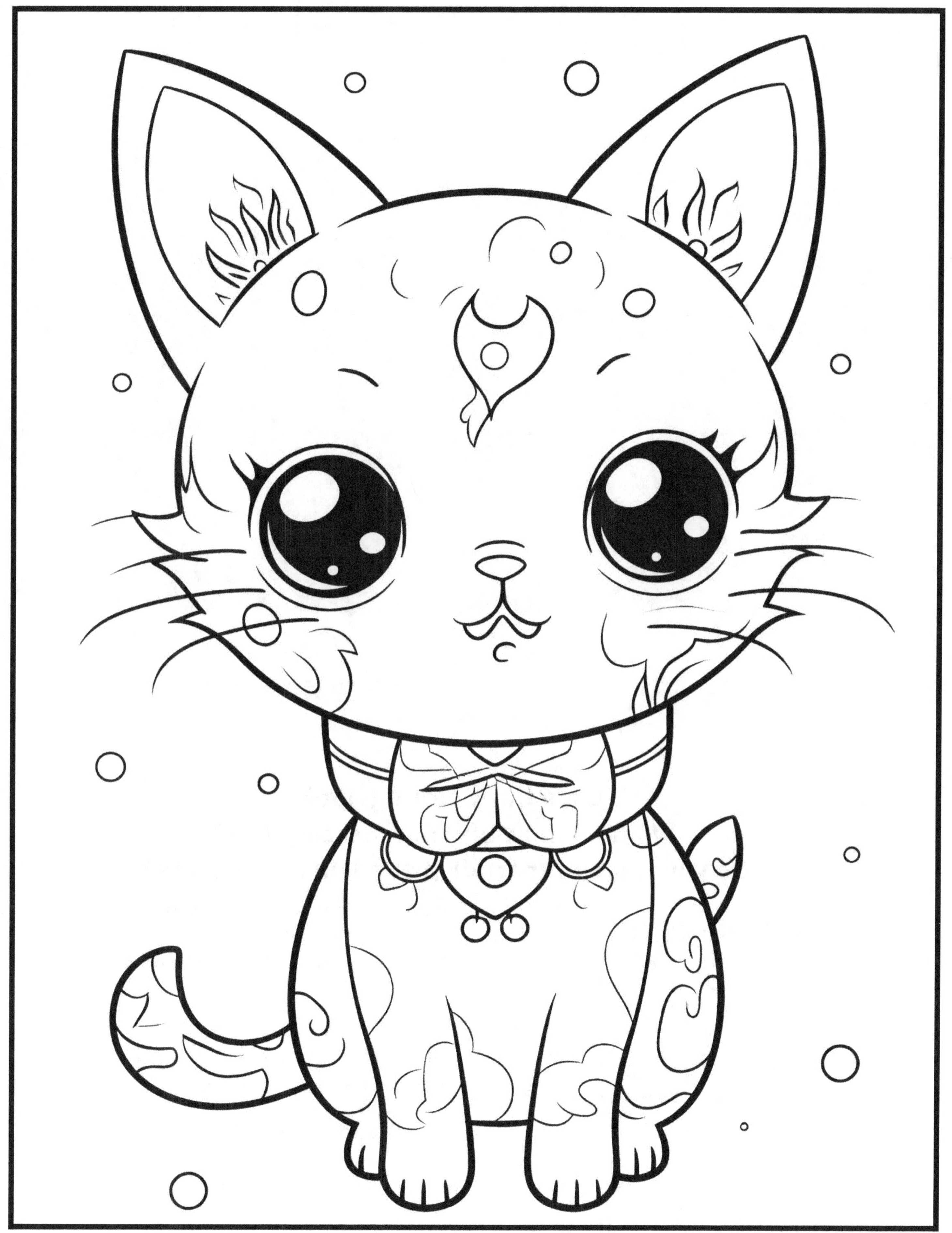

Love this Coloring book?
Want to show off your masterpiece?
Do you want your art displayed on our website?

1.   Take a picture of a finished coloring page
2.   Scan the QR Code to go to our website
3. Upload the photo of your finished coloring page

OR

Use #happytimesbooks or mention us
@happytimesbooks on Instragram to
have it displayed on our front page

No registration required

If you are under 18 please get a parents permission

https://happytimesbooks.com/pages/customer-art

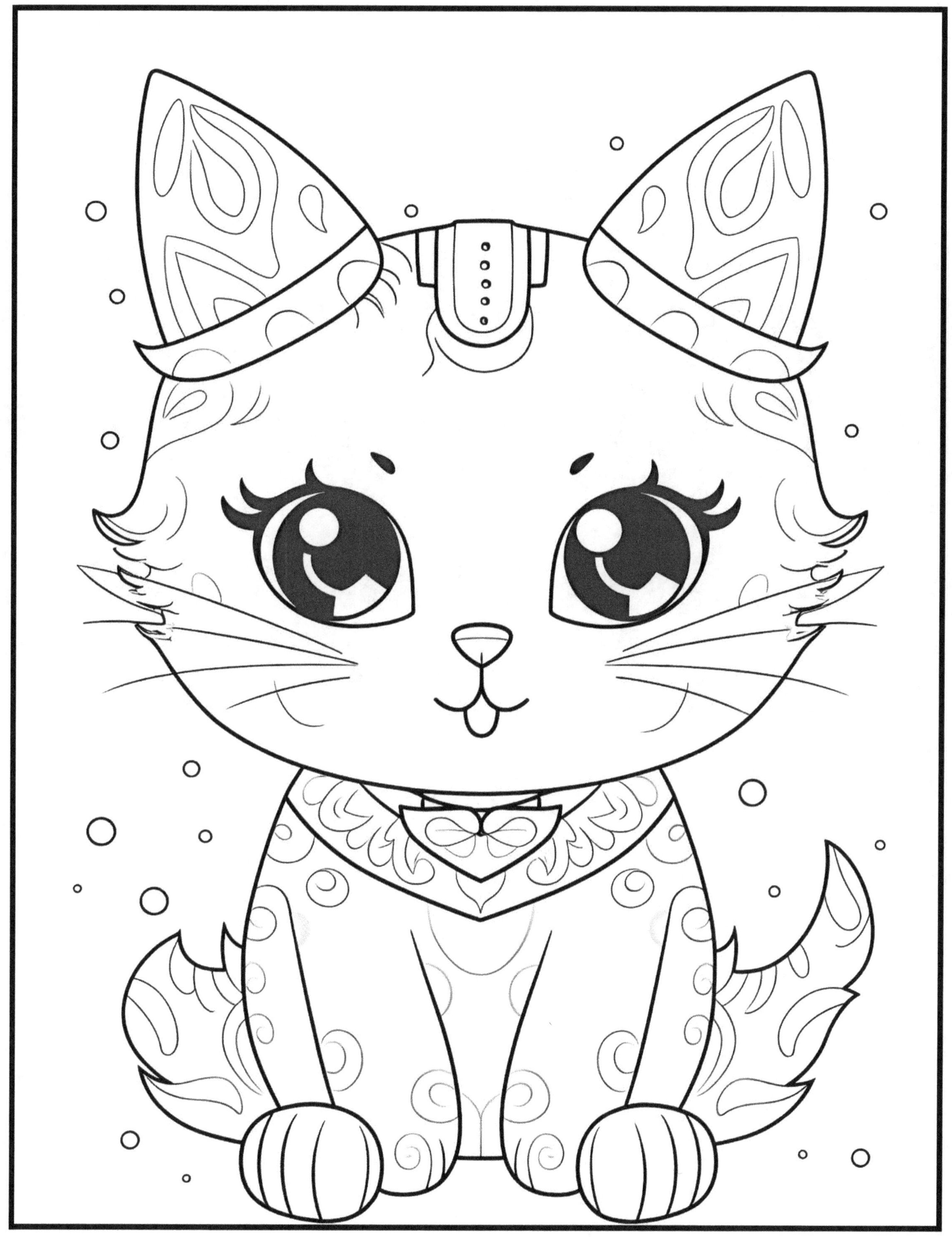

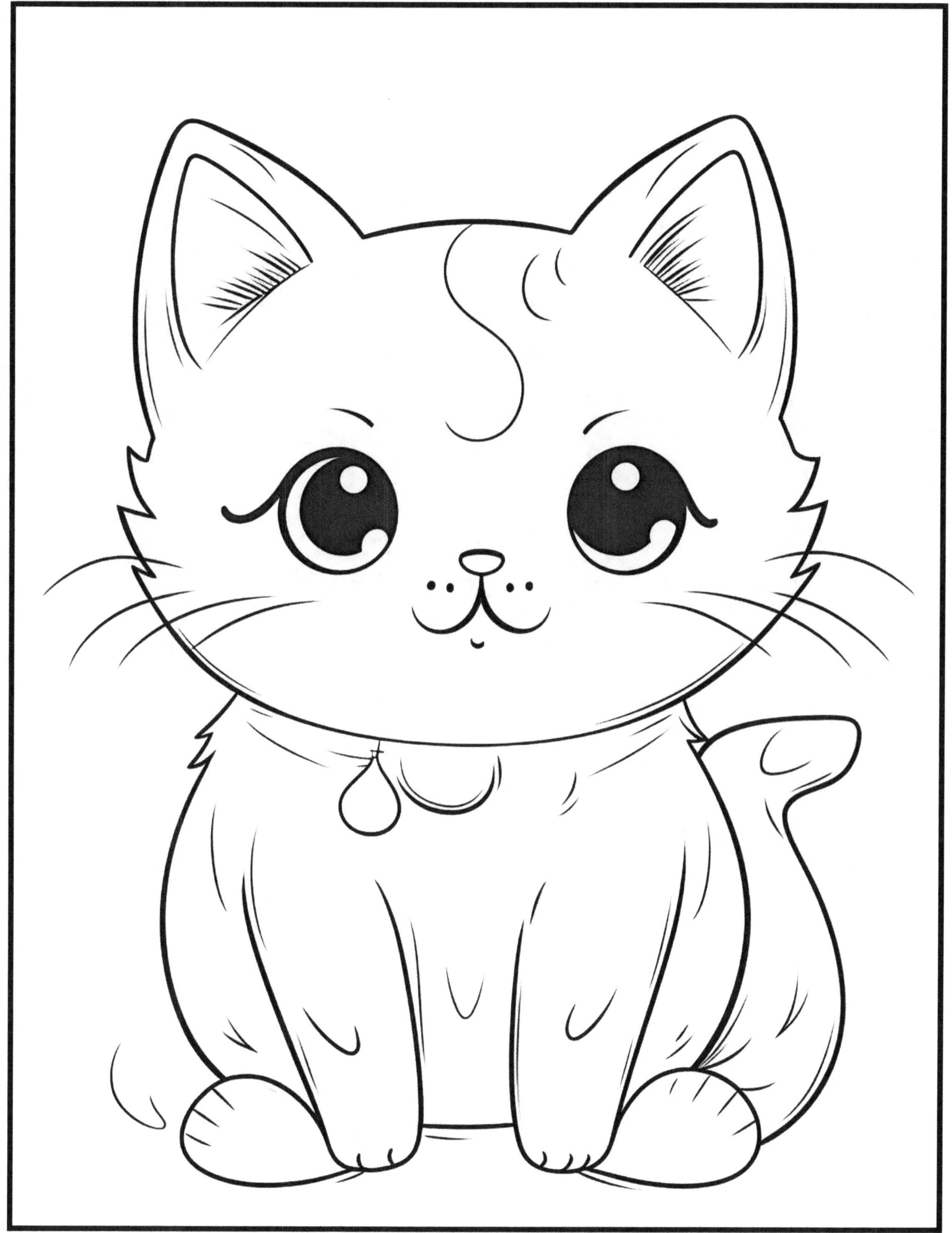

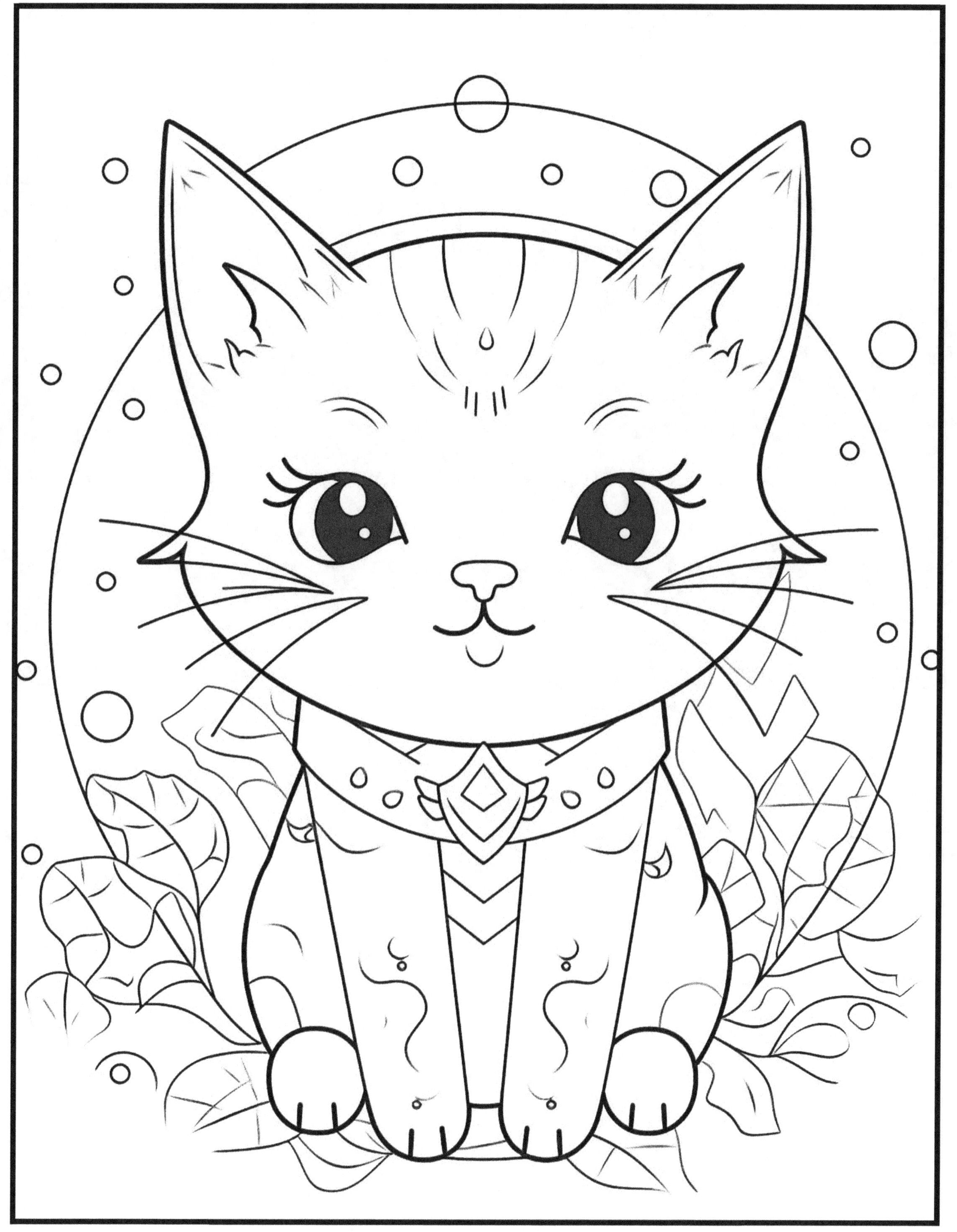

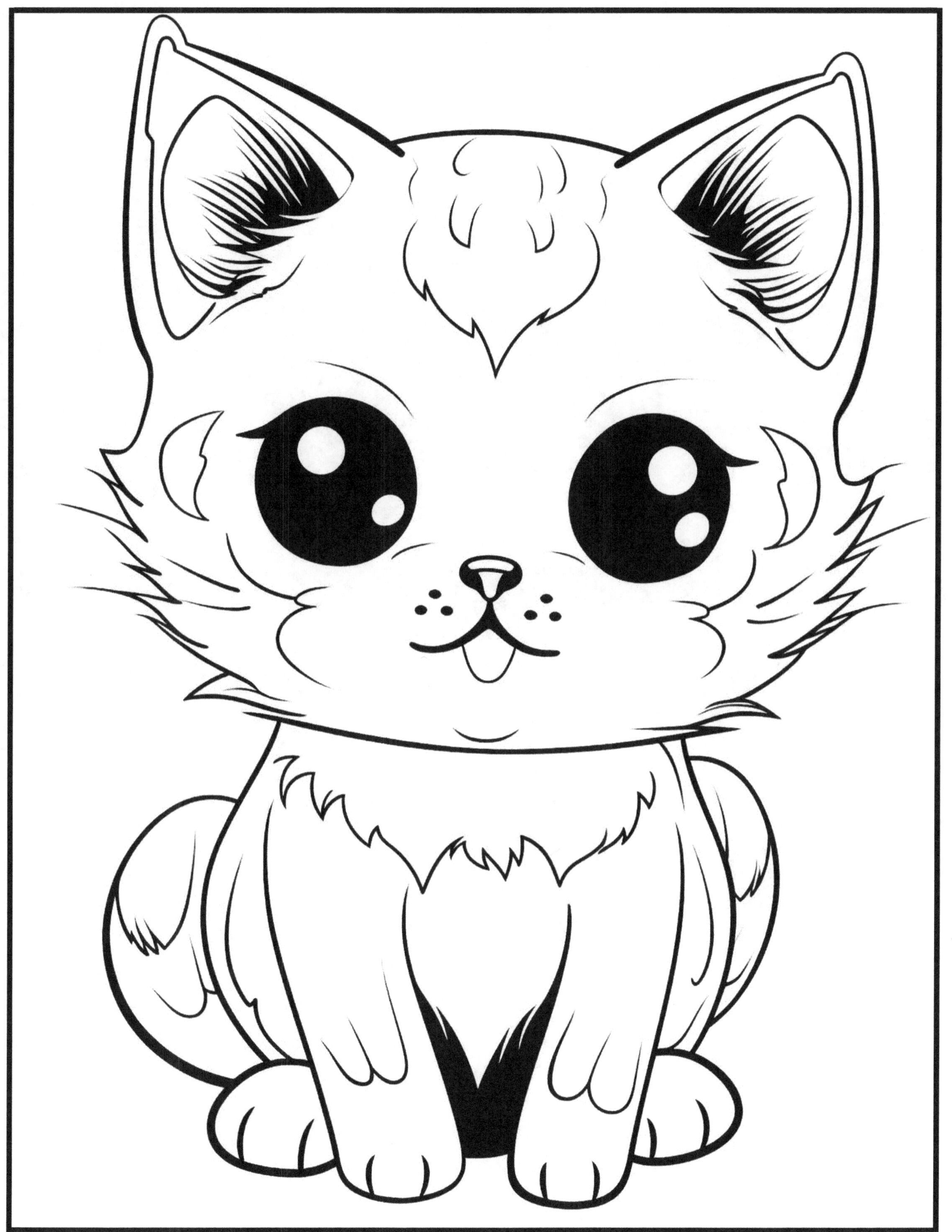

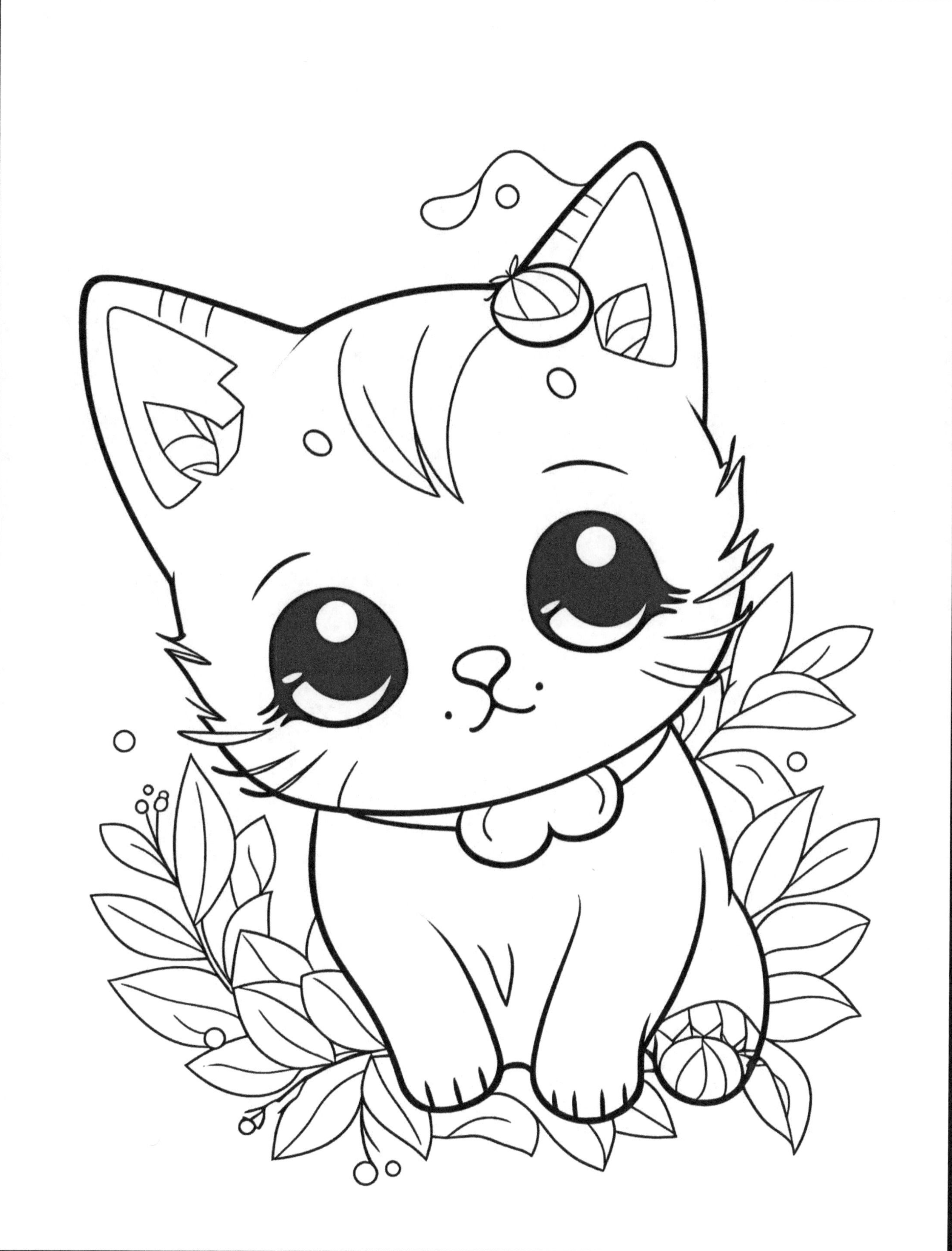

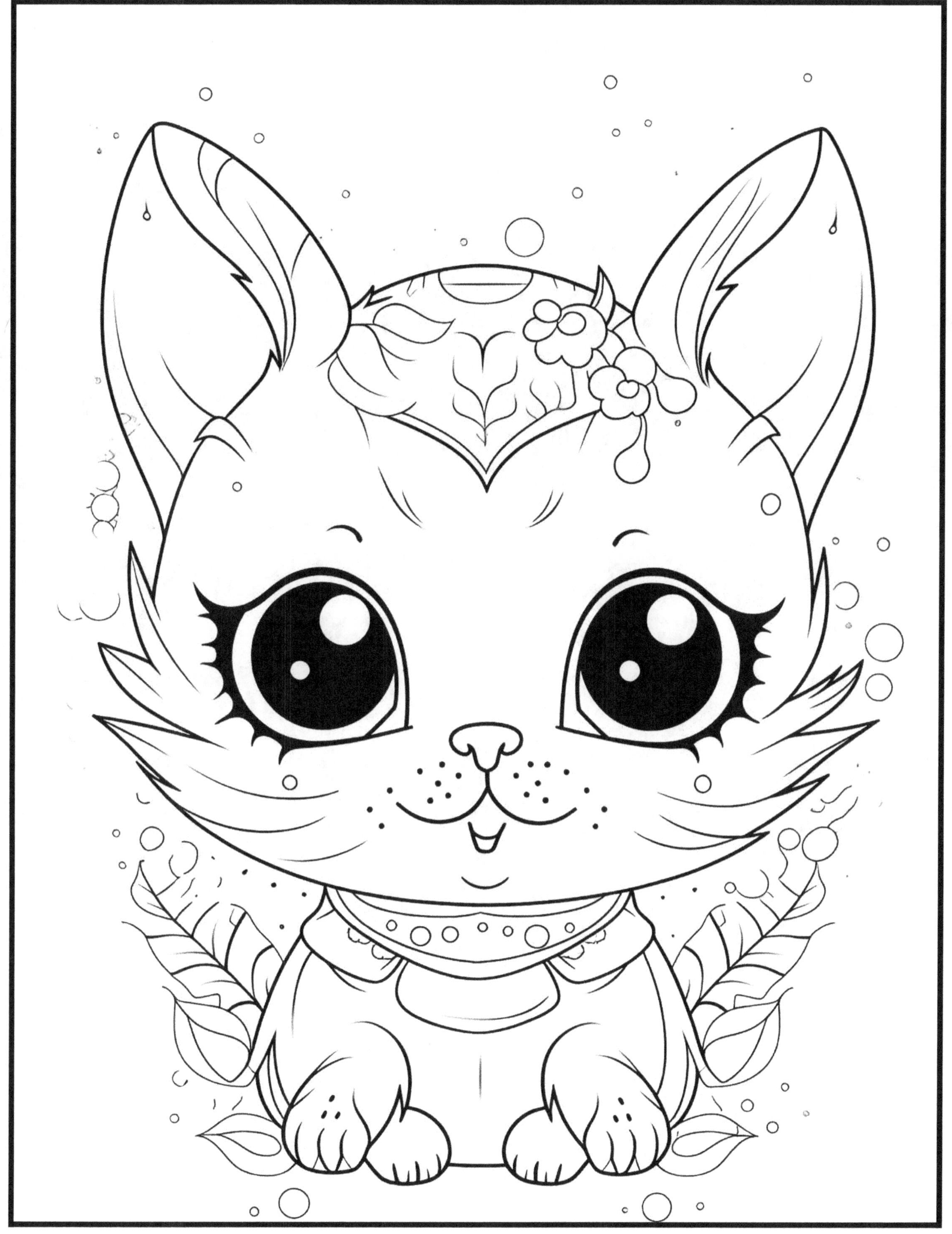

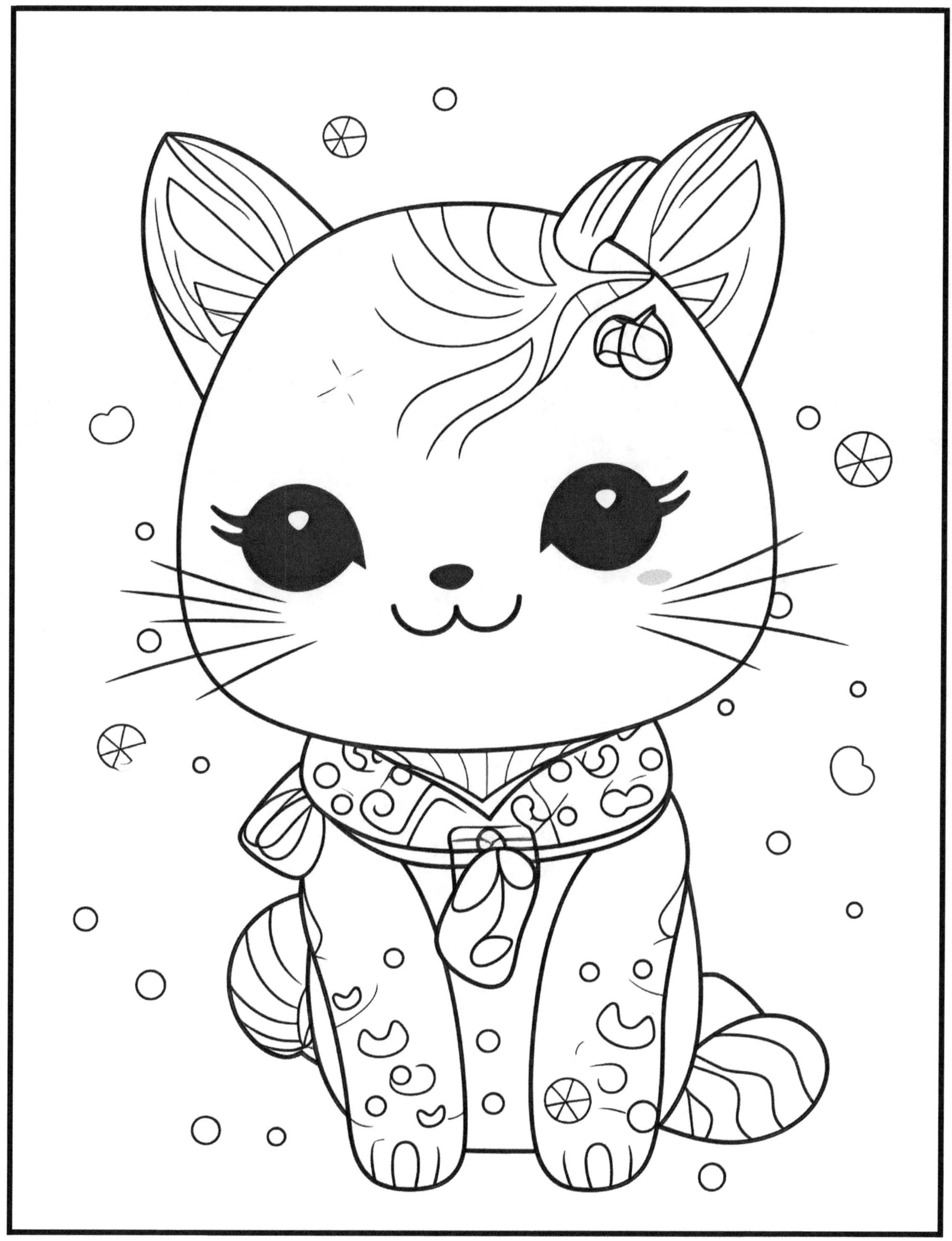

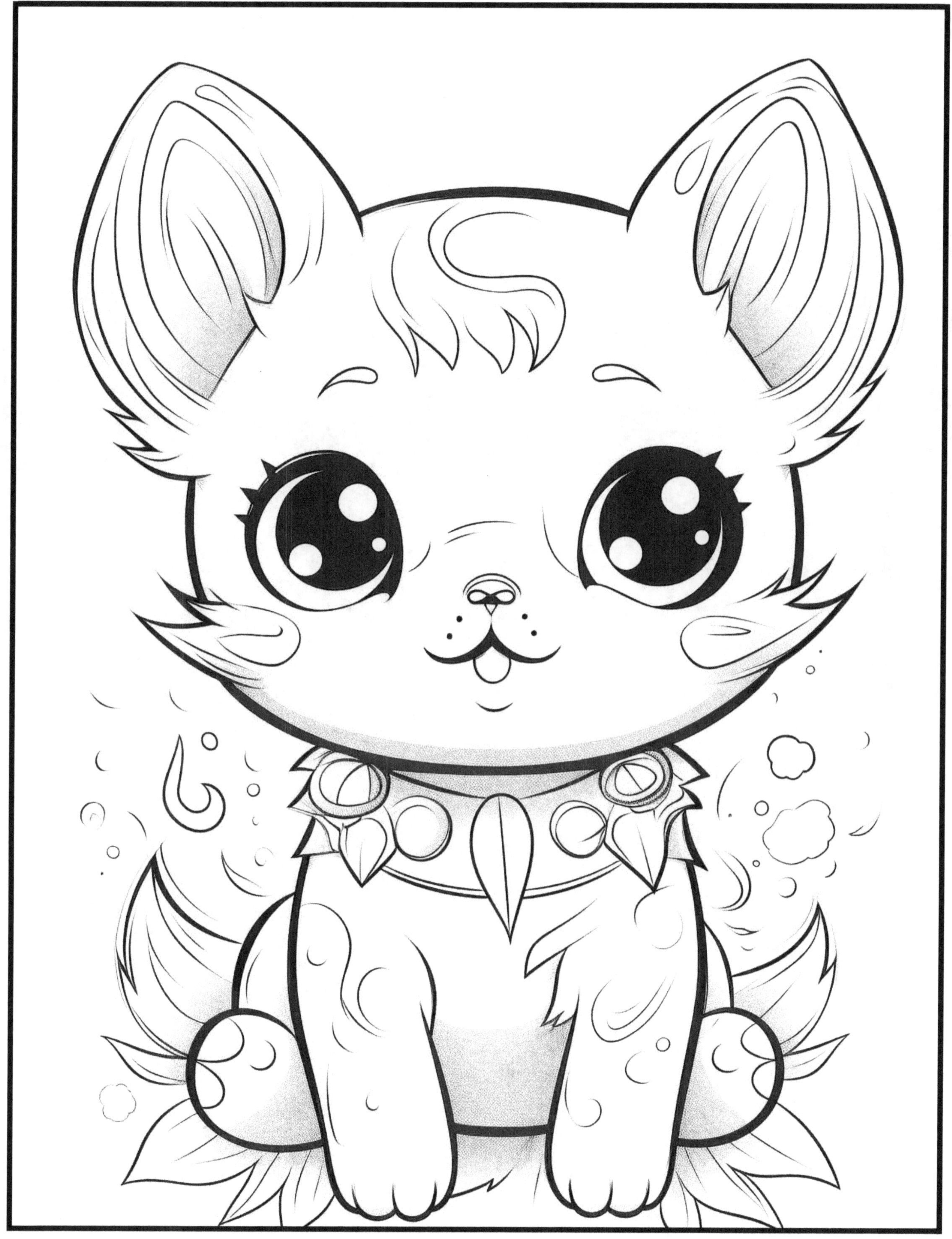

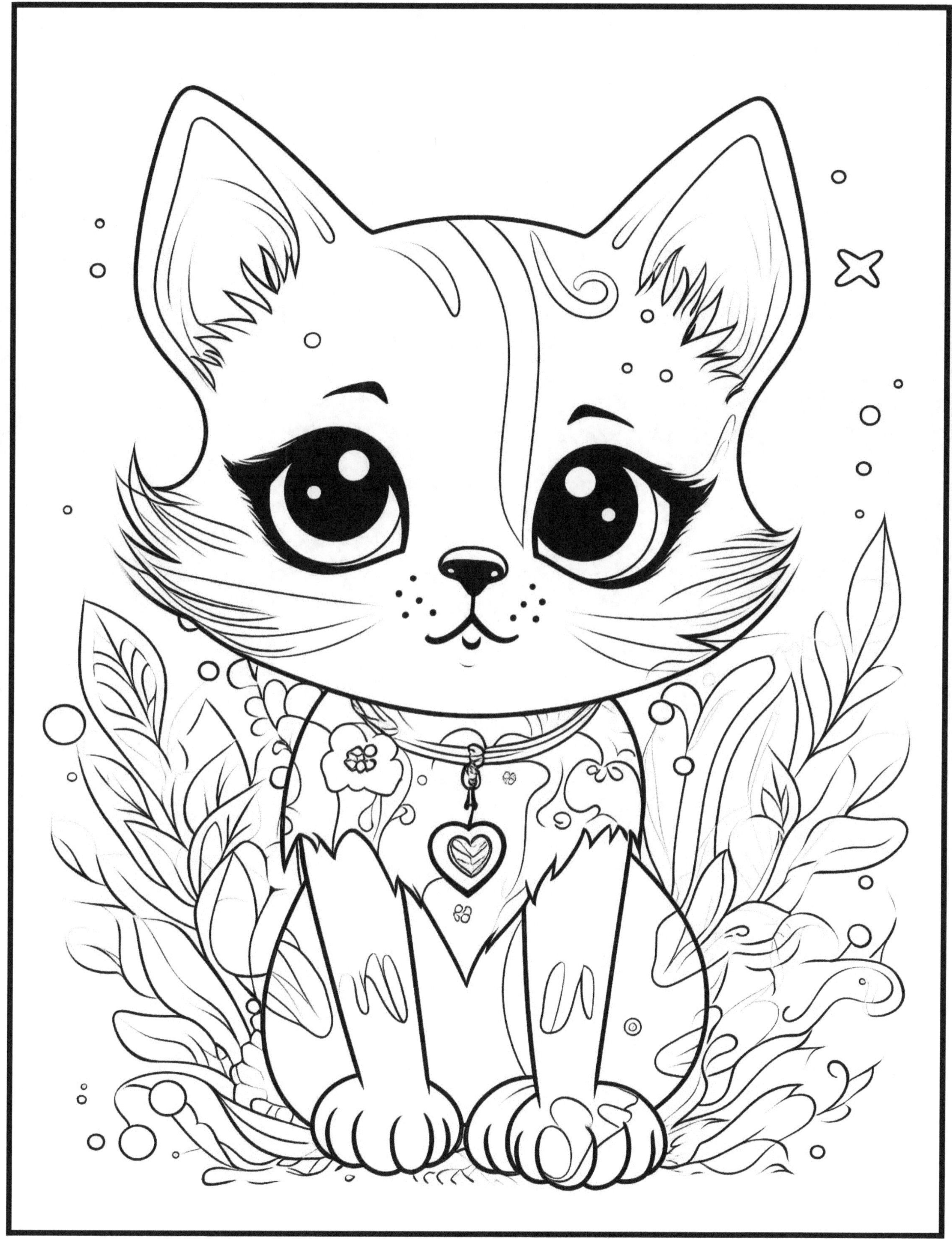

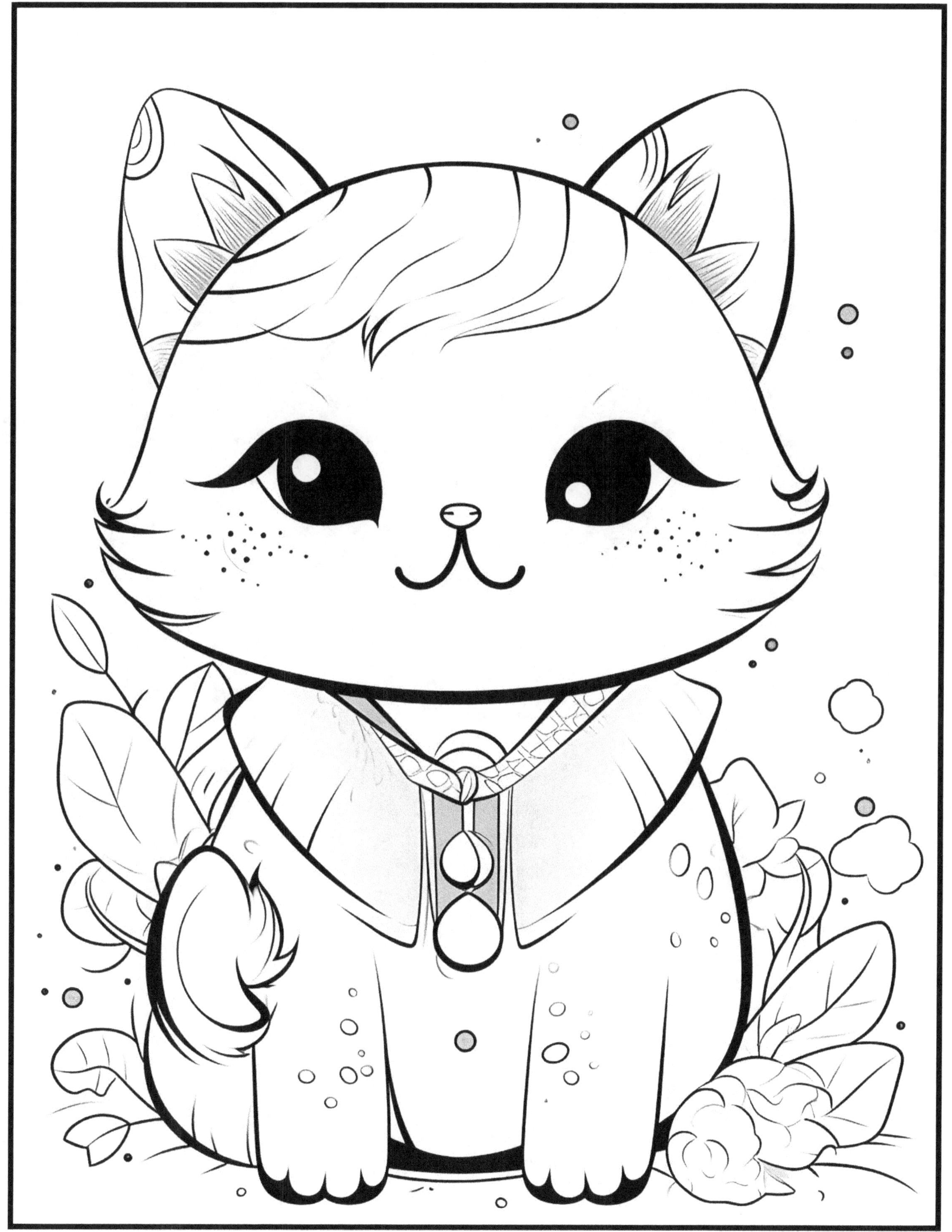

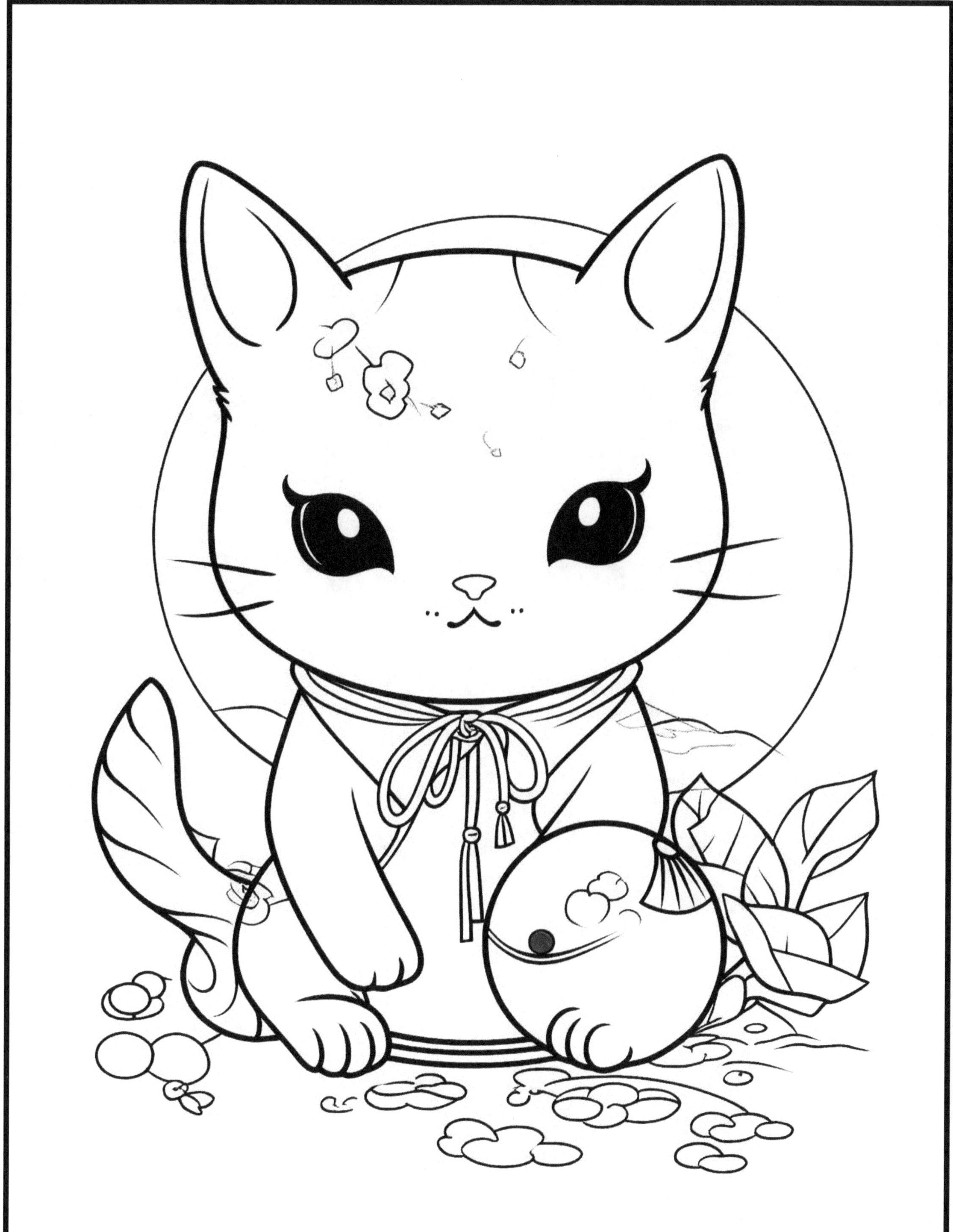

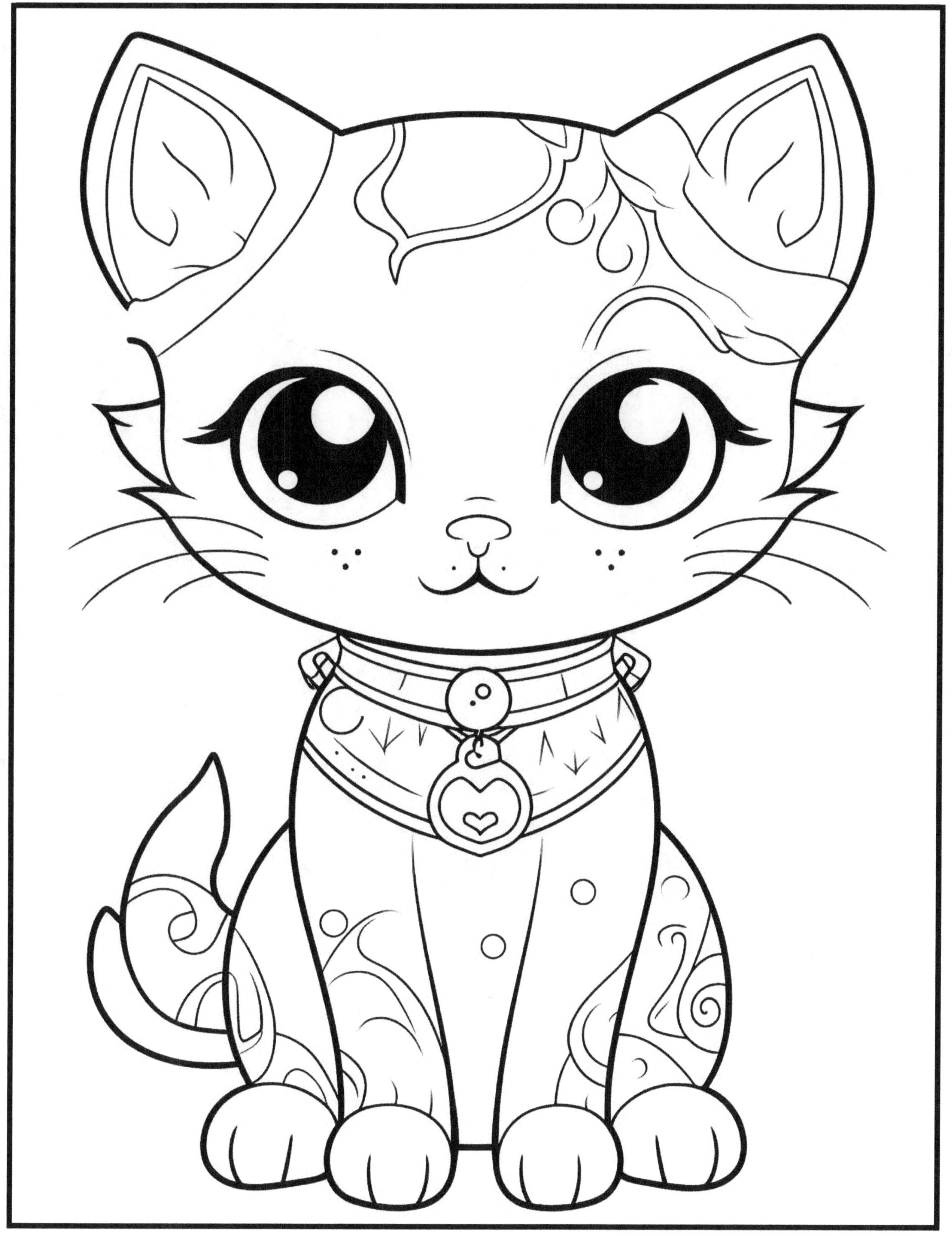

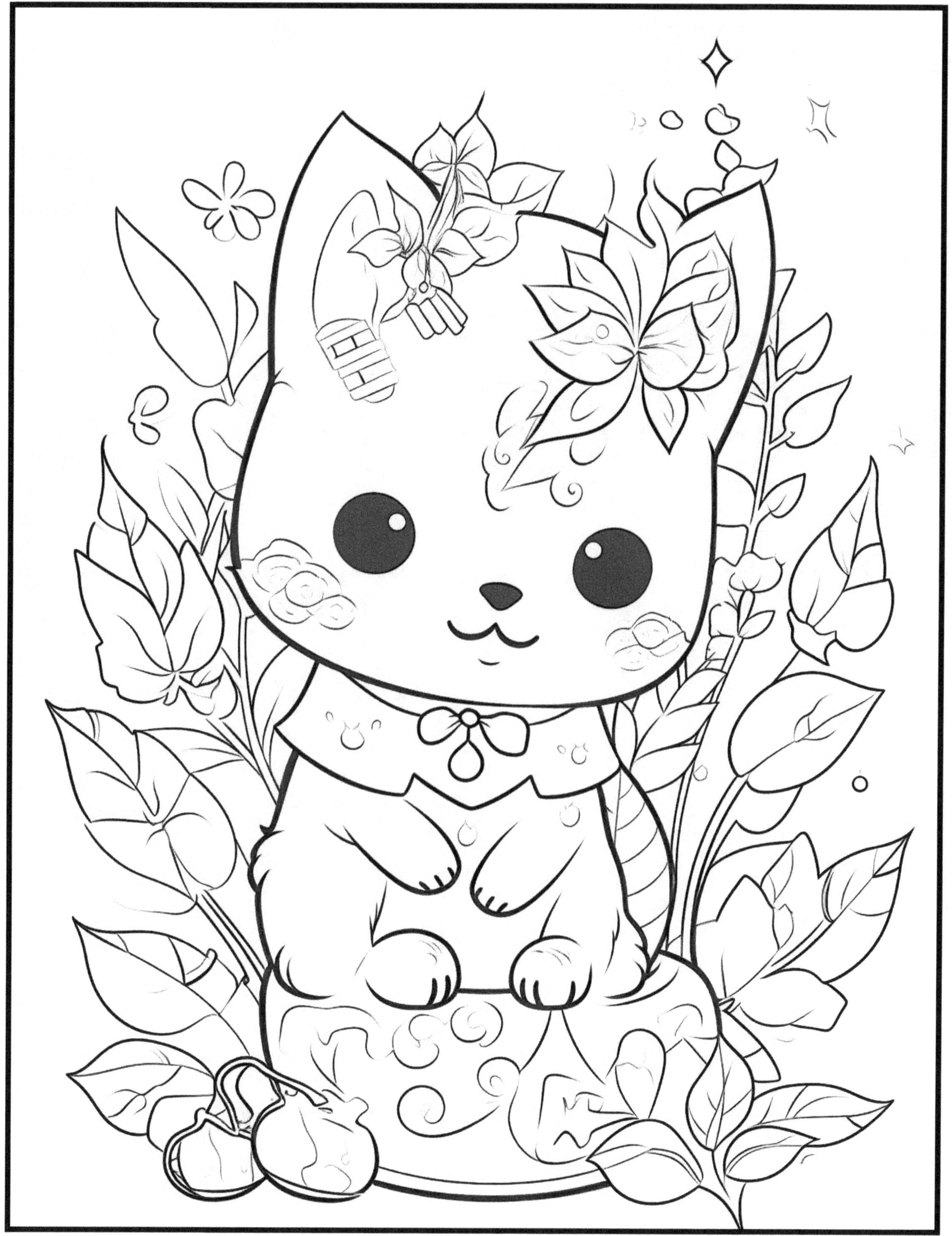

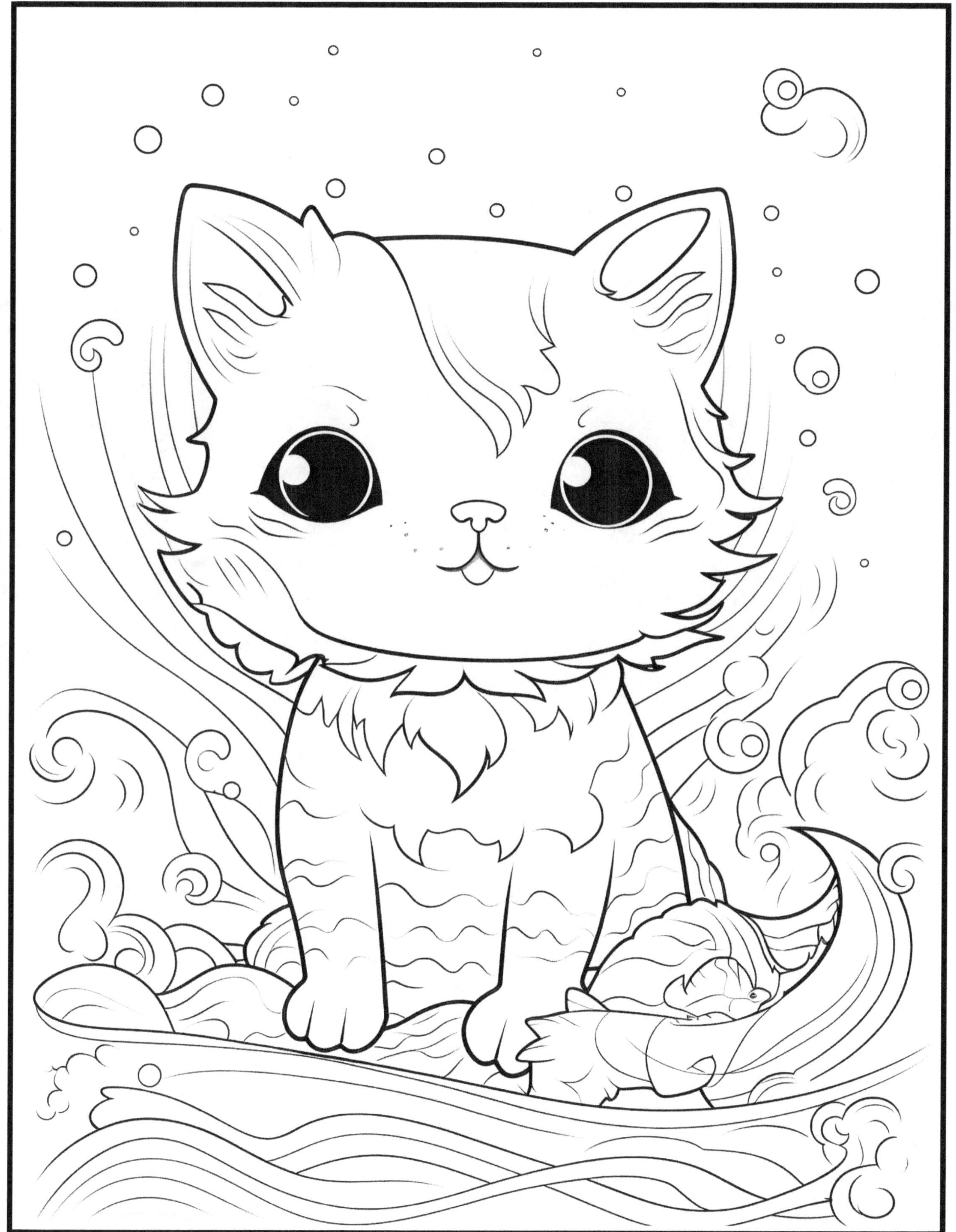

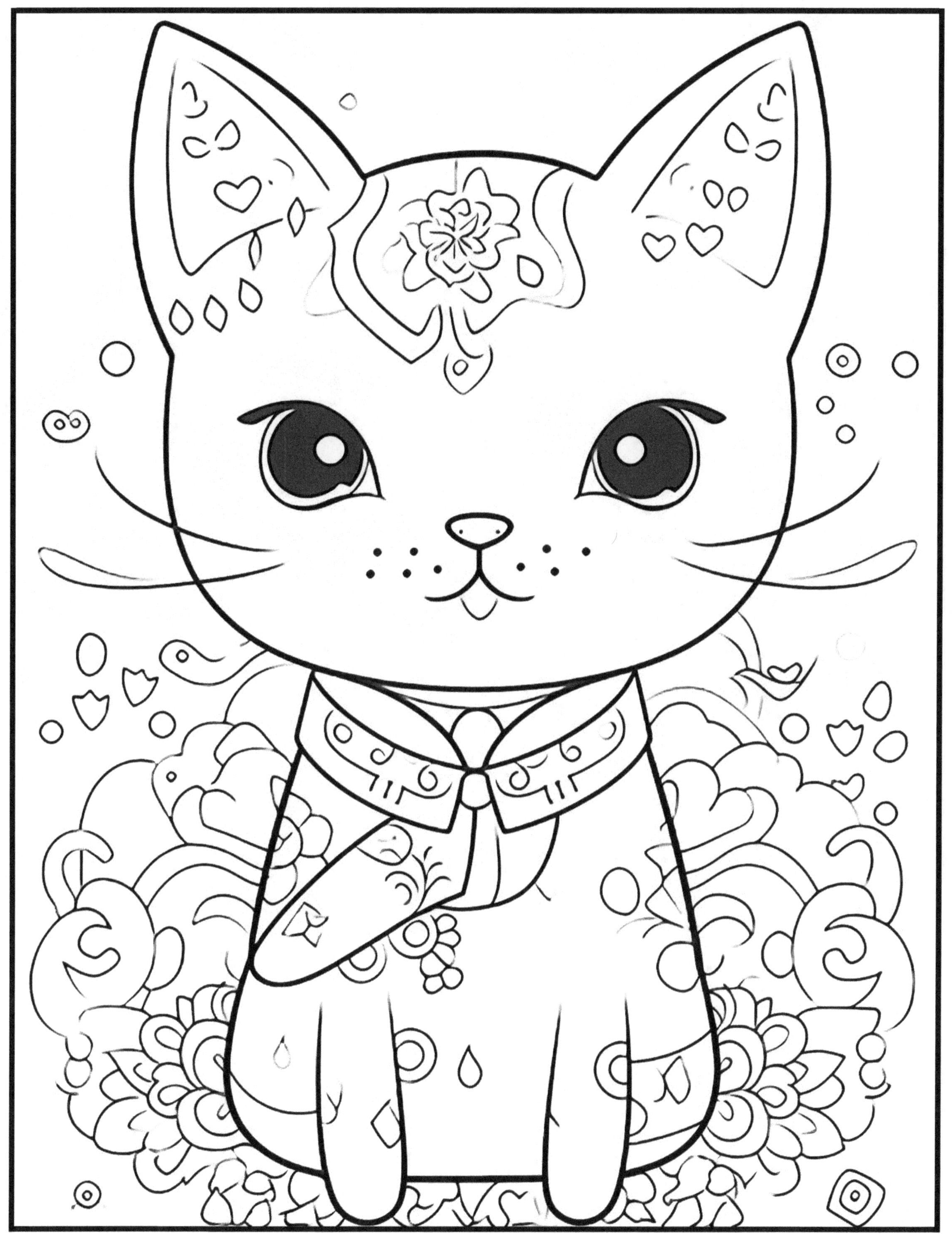

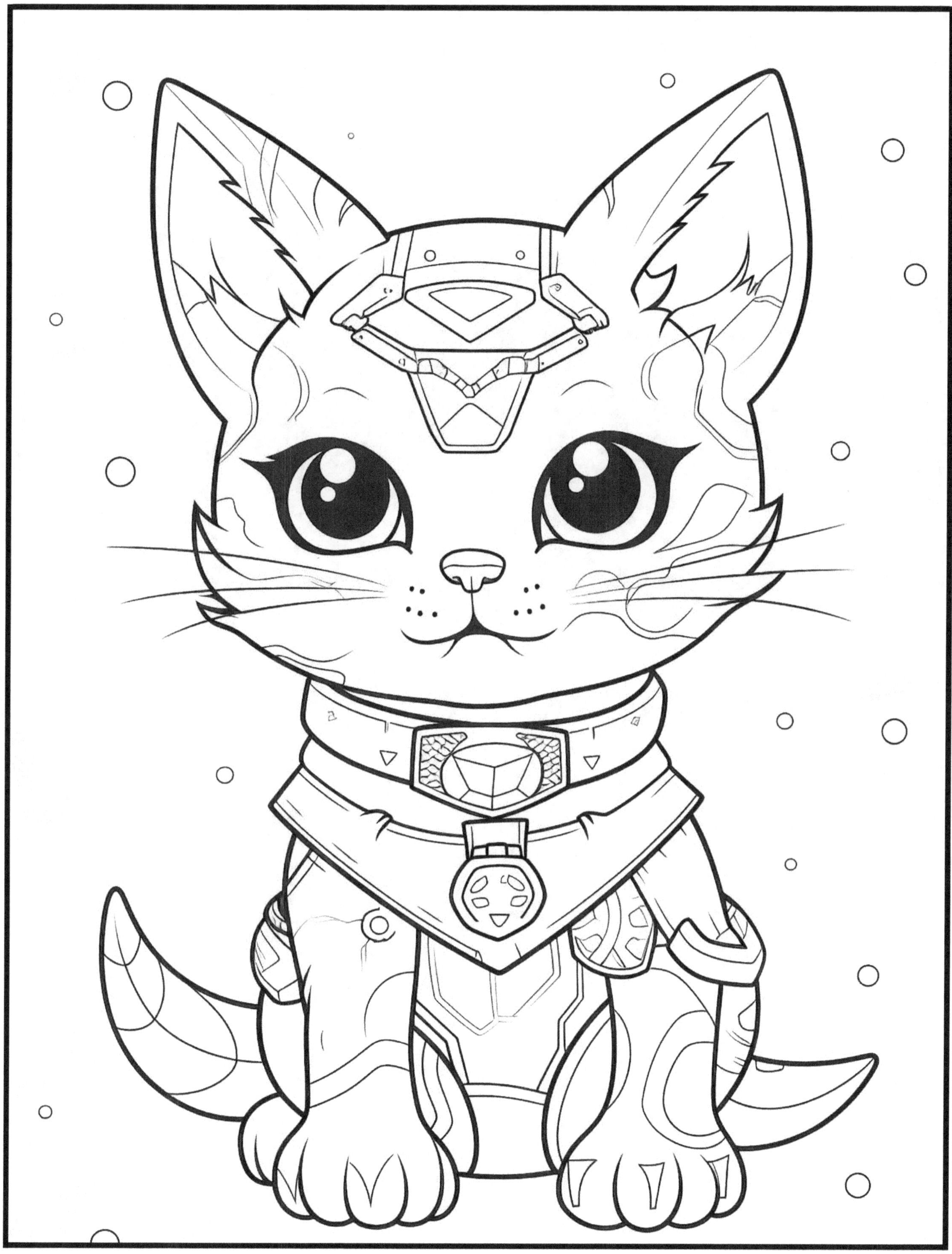

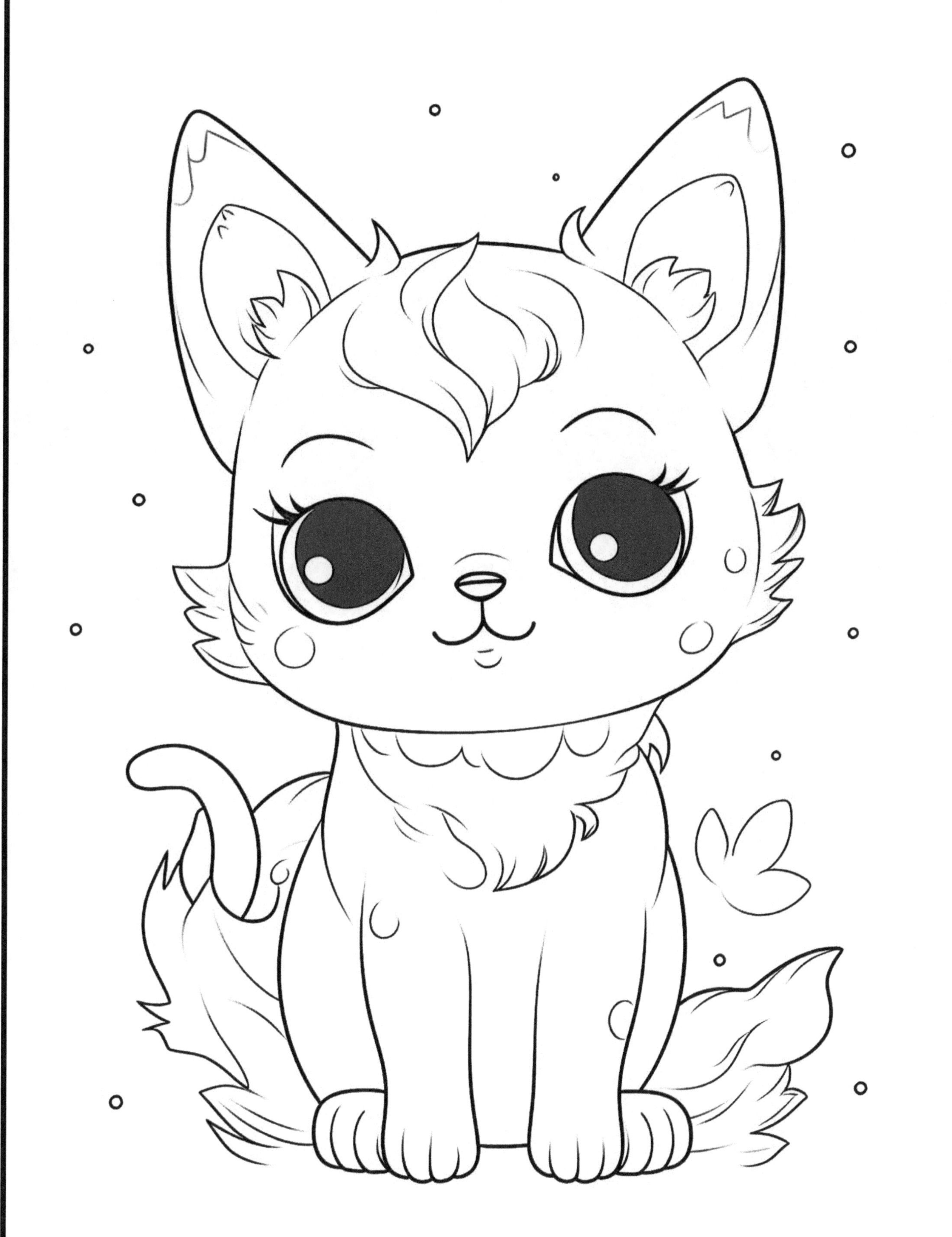

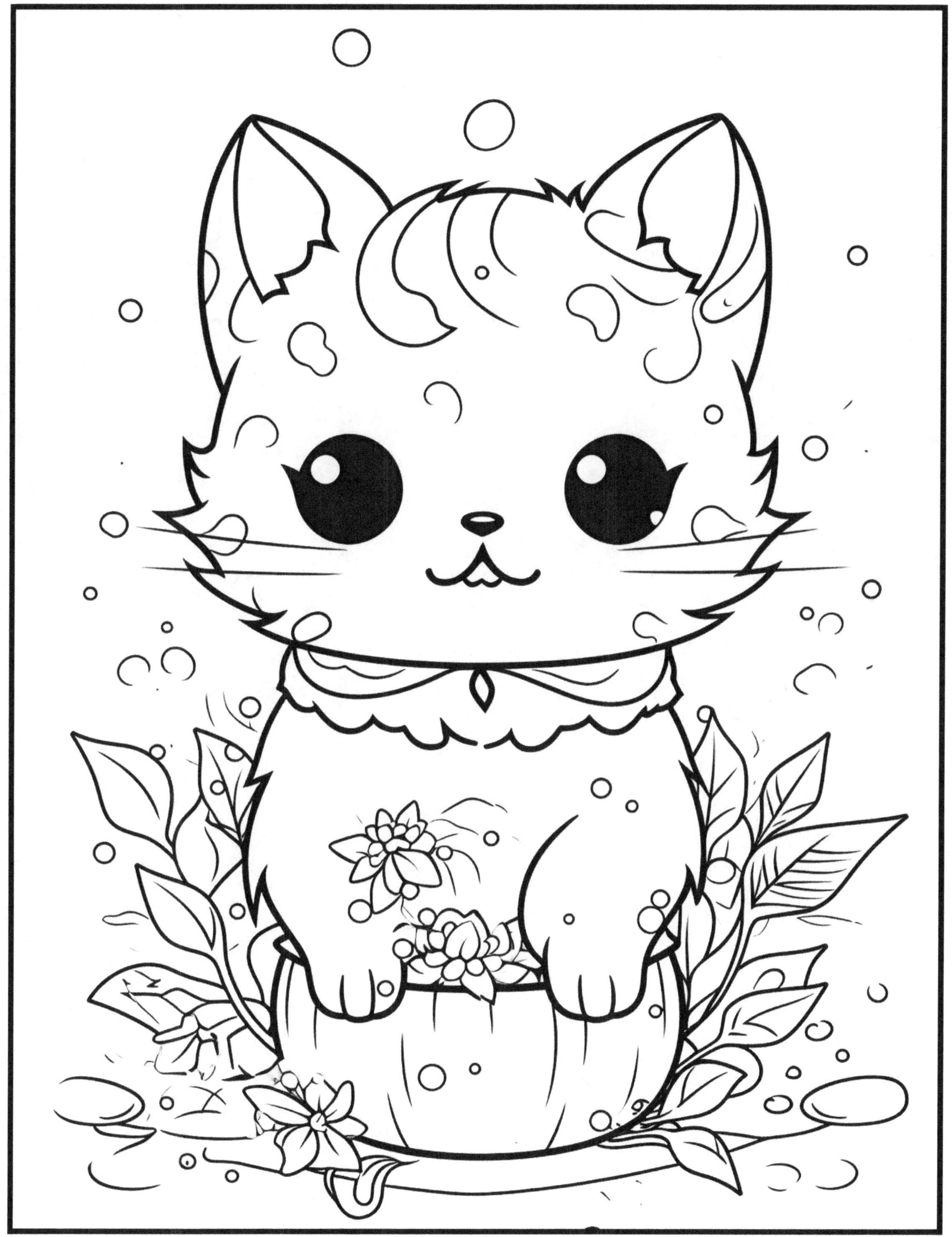

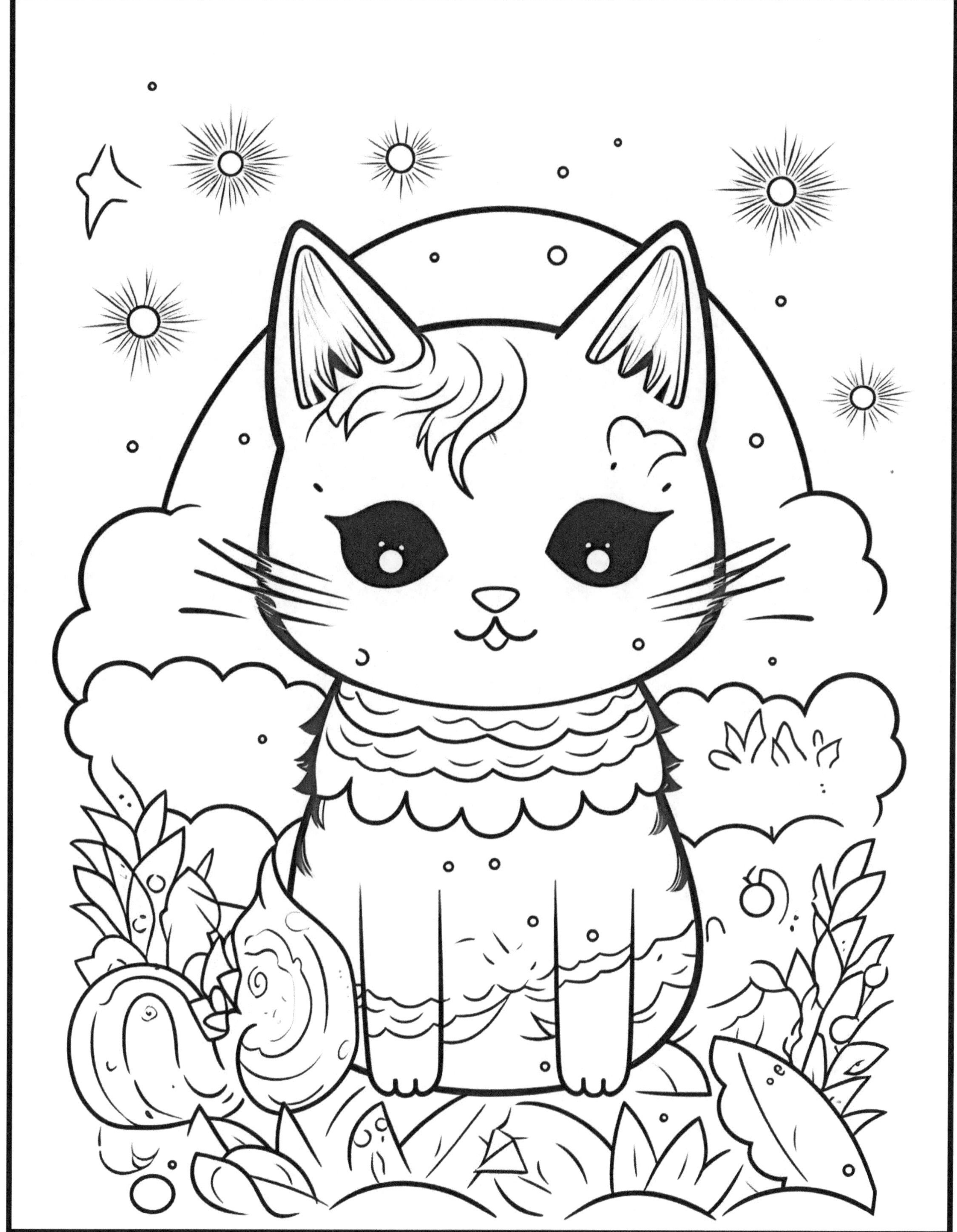

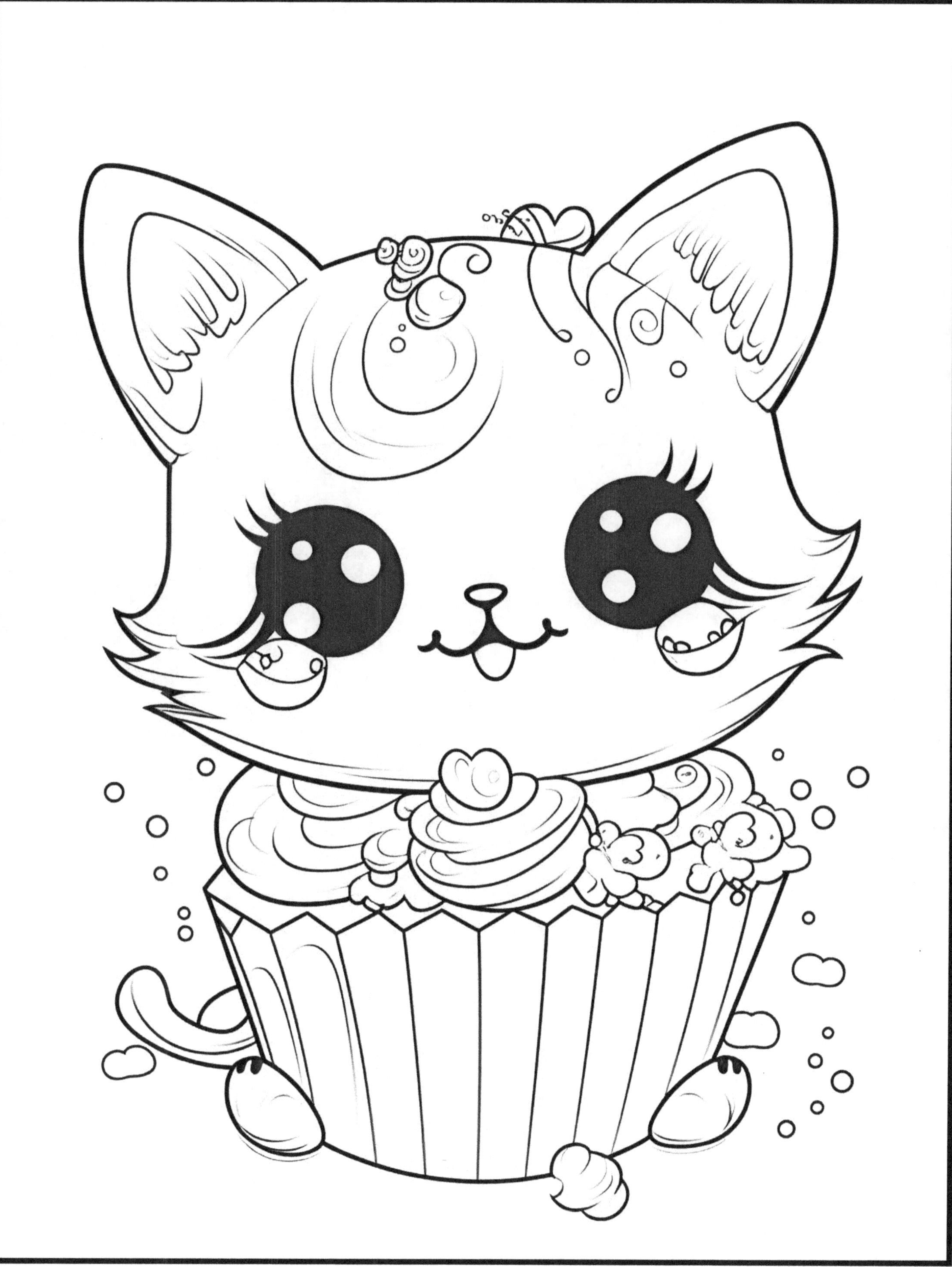

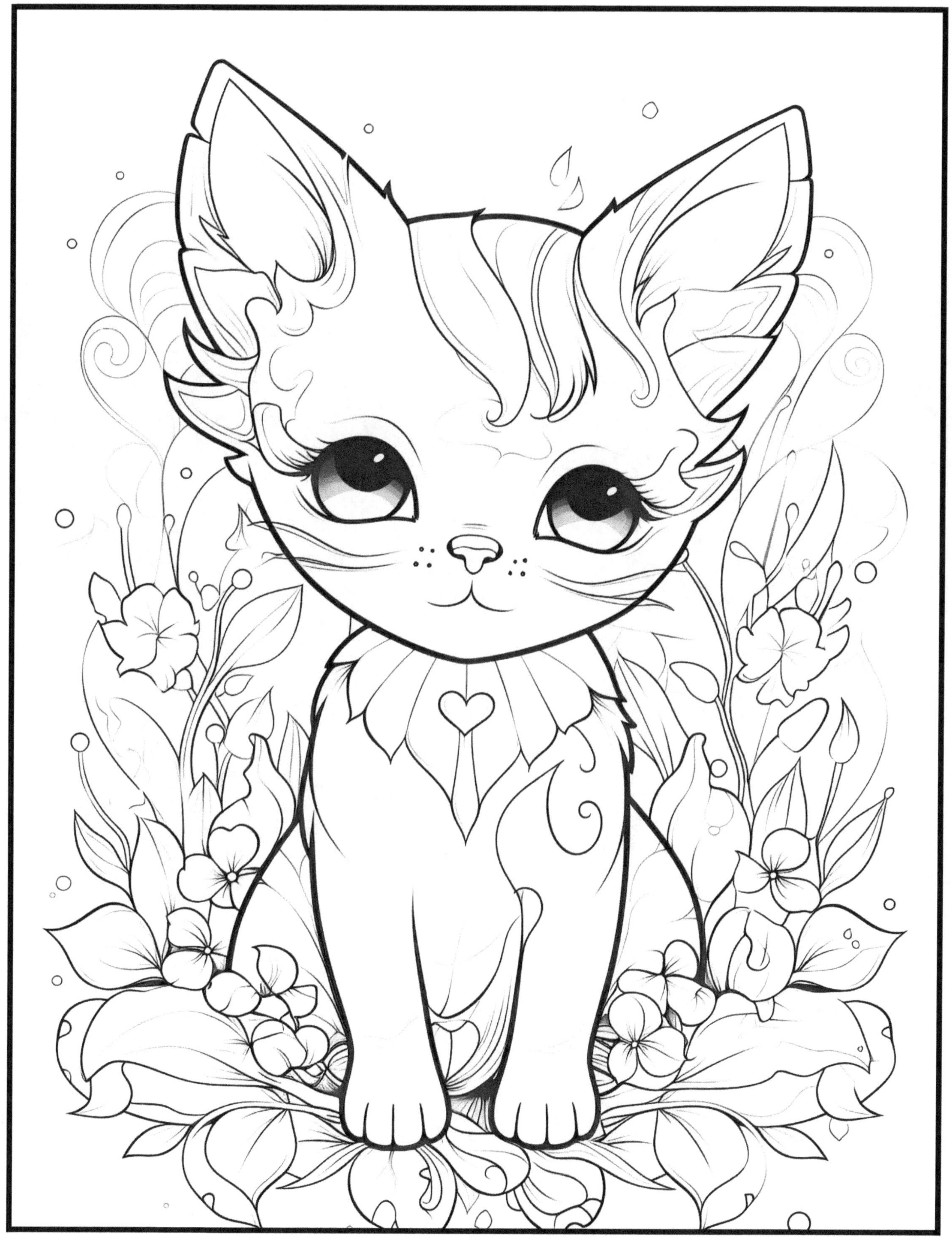

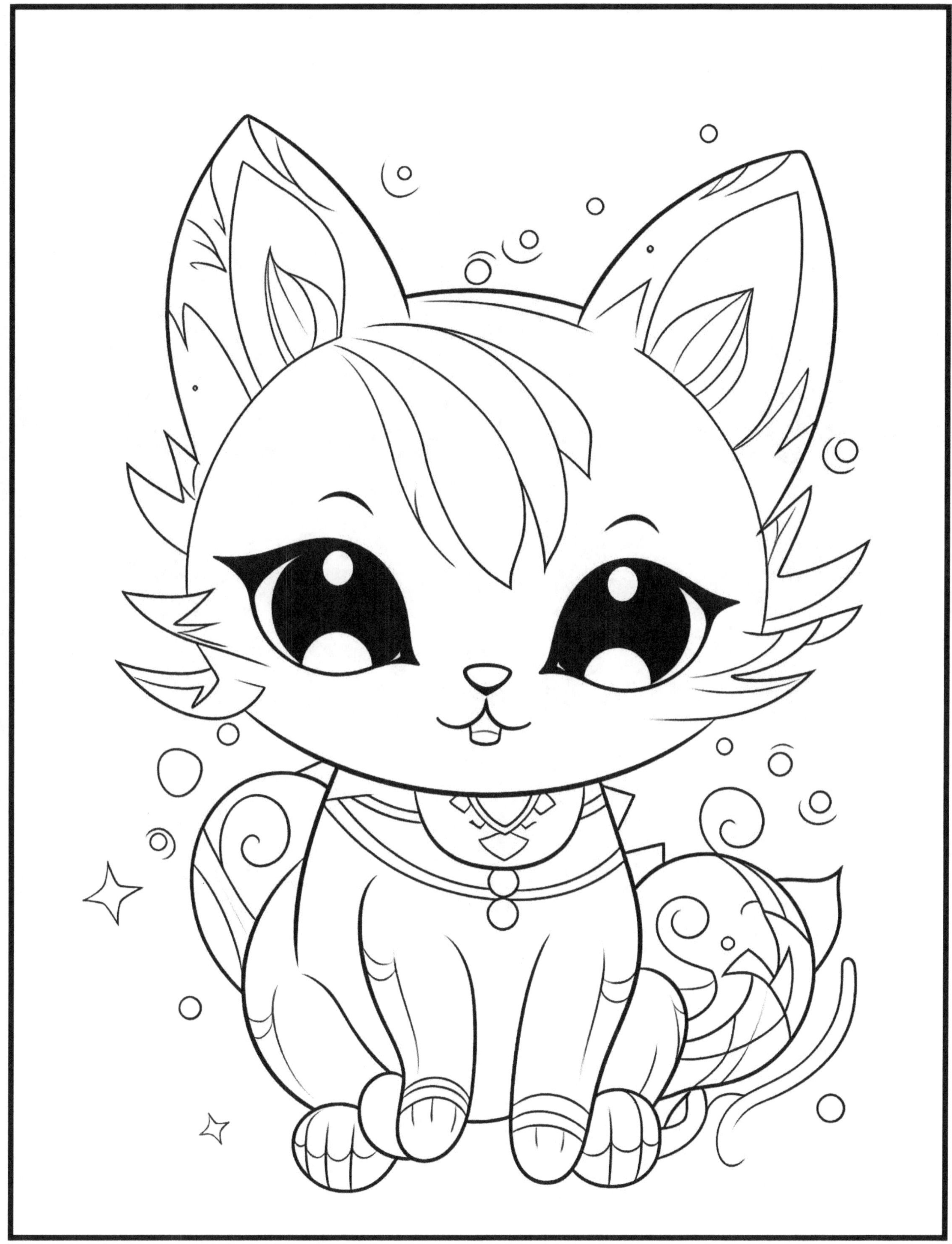

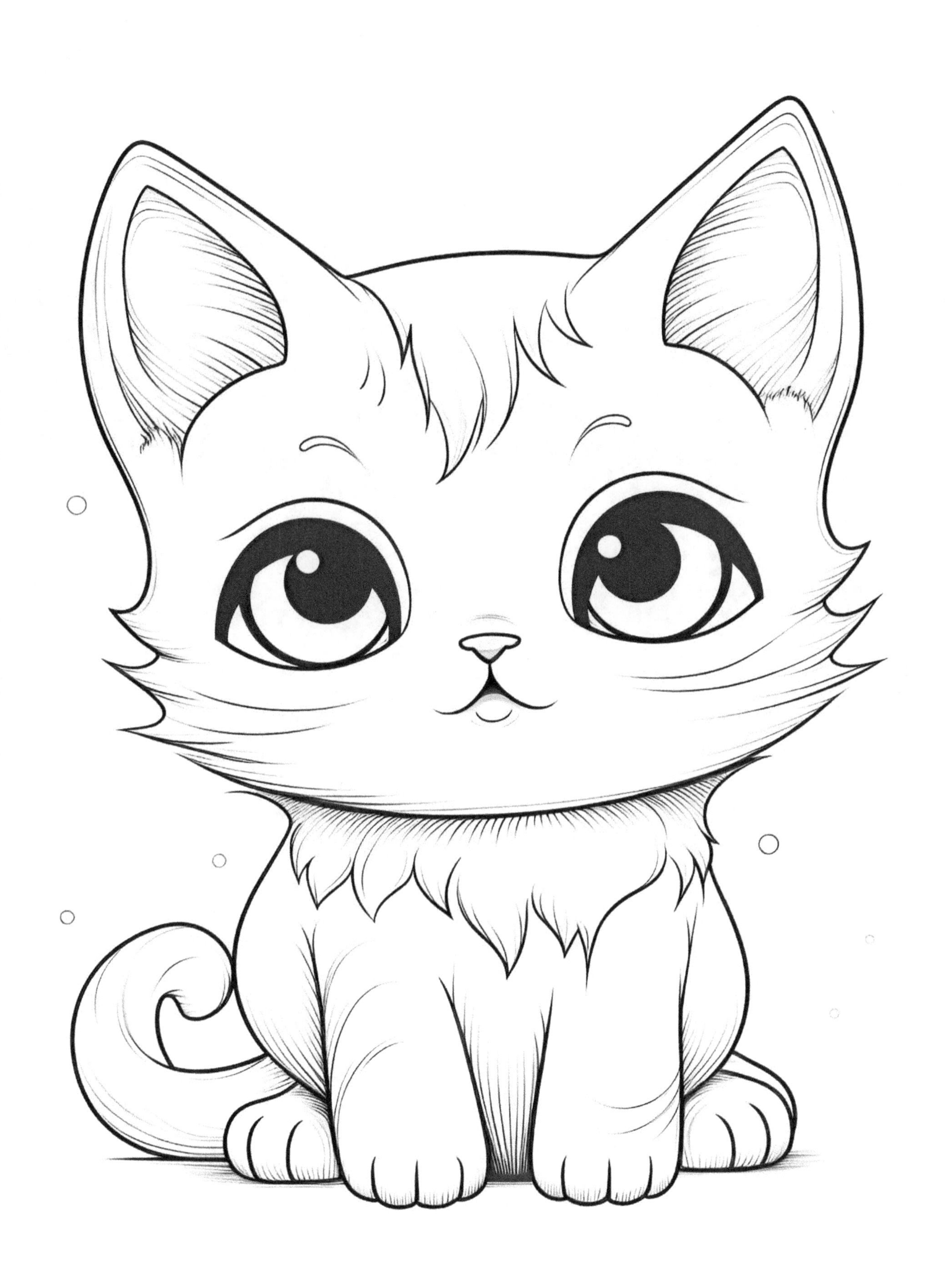

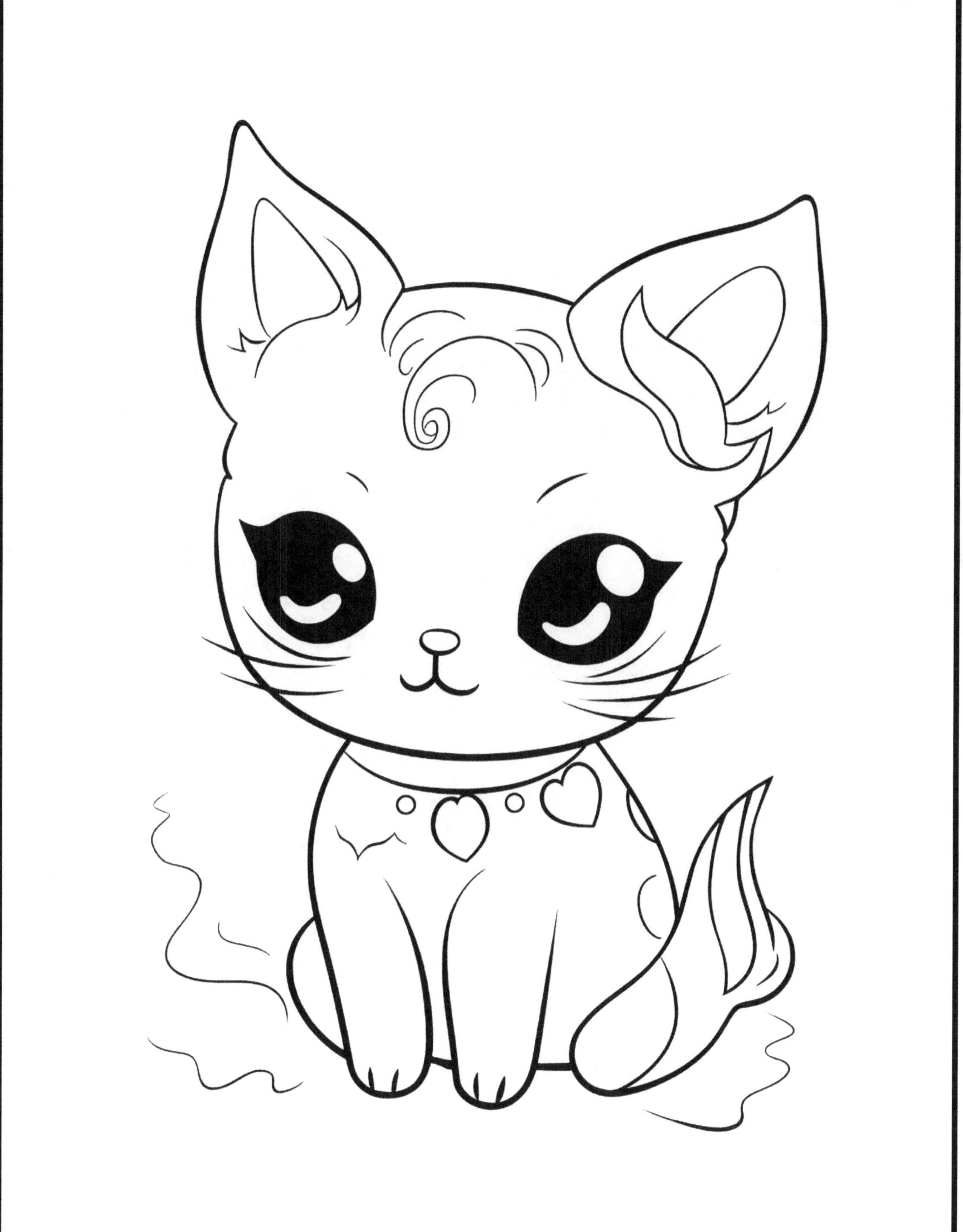

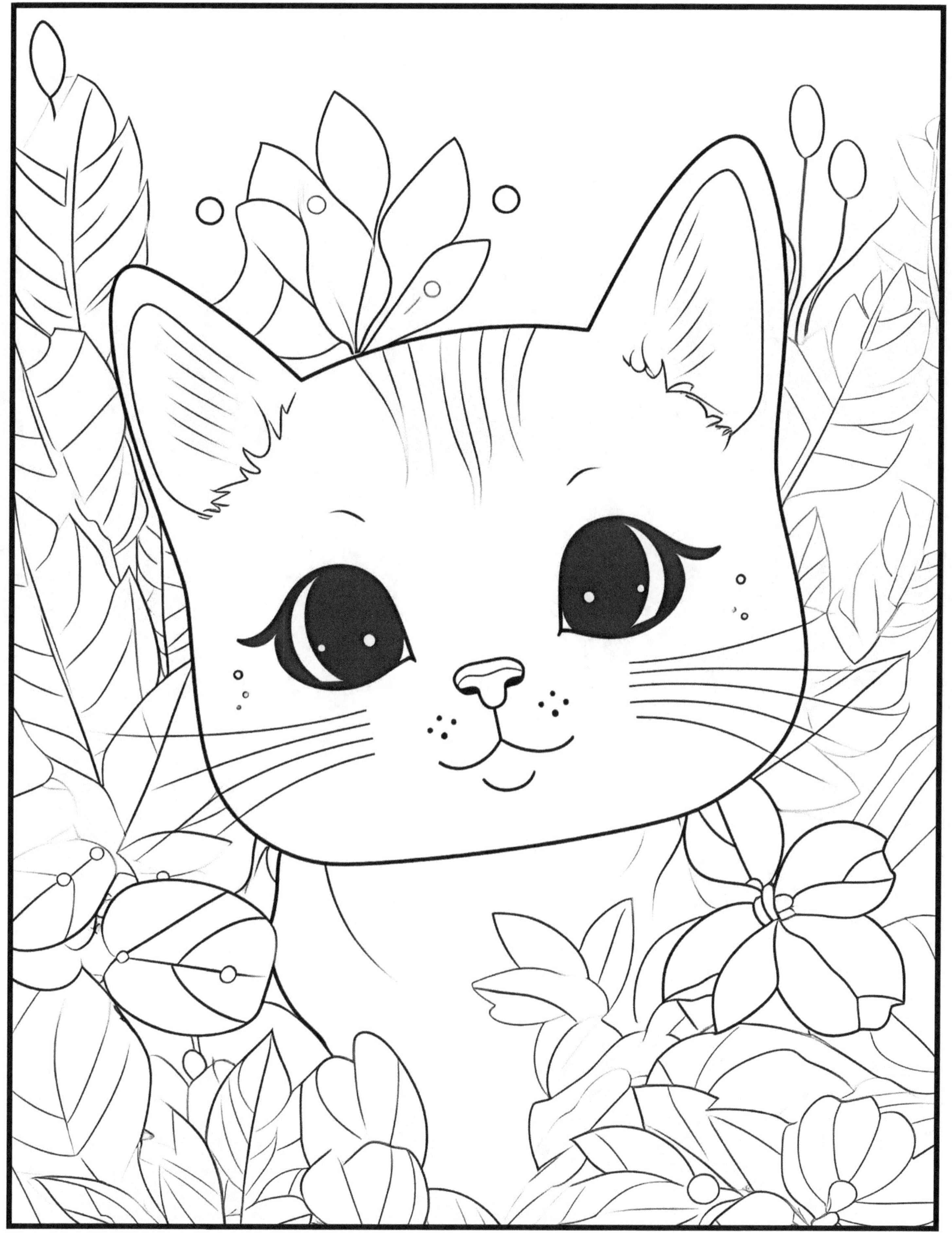

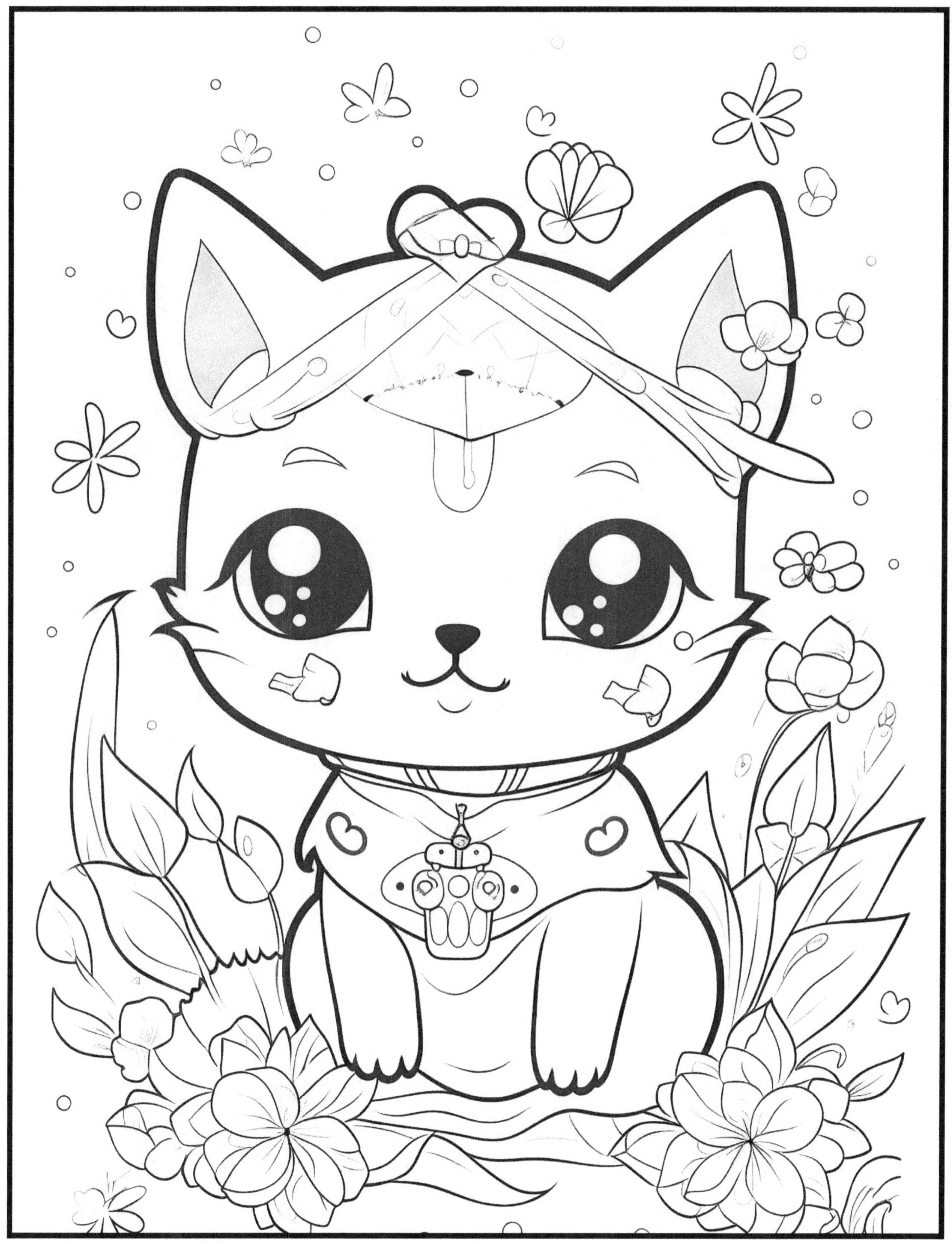

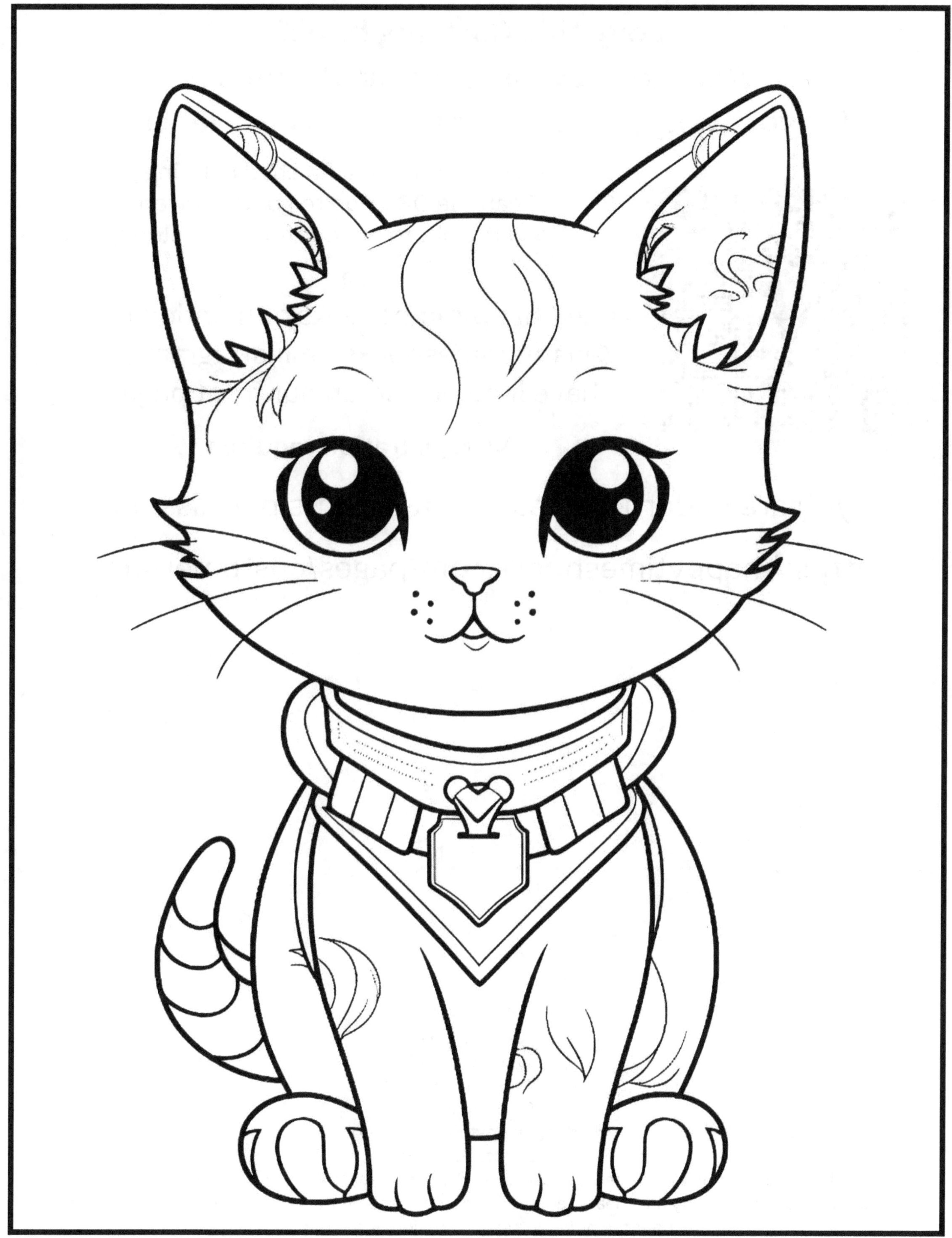

Love this Coloring book?
Want to show off your masterpiece?
Do you want your art displayed on our website?

1.   Take a picture of a finished coloring page
2.   Scan the QR Code to go to our website
3. Upload the photo of your finished coloring page

OR
Use #happytimesbooks or mention us
@happytimesbooks on Instragram to
have it displayed on our front page

No registration required

If you are under 18 please get a parents permission

https://happytimesbooks.com/pages/customer-art